VIKINGS

Casemate Short History

VIKINGS

RAIDERS FROM THE SEA

Kim Hjardar

CASEMATE
Oxford & Philadelphia

Published in Great Britain and
the United States of America in 2017 by
CASEMATE PUBLISHERS
The Old Music Hall, 106–108 Cowley Road, Oxford OX4 1JE, UK
1950 Lawrence Road, Havertown, PA 19083, USA

Paperback Edition: ISBN 978-1-61200-519-5
Digital Edition: ISBN 978-1-61200-520-1 (epub)

A CIP record for this book is available from the British Library

Printed in the Czech Republic by FINIDR, s.r.o.
Typeset in India by Lapiz Digital Services, Chennai

For a complete list of Casemate titles, please contact:

CASEMATE PUBLISHERS (UK)
Telephone (01865) 241249
Email: casemate-uk@casematepublishers.co.uk
www.casematepublishers.co.uk

CASEMATE PUBLISHERS (US)
Telephone (610) 853-9131
Fax (610) 853-9146
Email: casemate@casematepublishers.com
www.casematepublishers.com

CONTENTS

INTRODUCTION

FROM THE 9TH TO THE 11TH CENTURY, Viking ships landed on almost every shore in the western world. Viking ravages united the Spanish kingdoms and stopped Charlemagne and the Franks' advance in Europe. Wherever Viking ships roamed, enormous suffering followed in their wake, but the encounter between cultures changed both European and Nordic societies. Employing sail technology and using unpredictable strategies, the Vikings could strike suddenly, attack with great force, then withdraw with stolen goods or captives. This short history of the Vikings discusses their society and unique way of life, their ships, weapons and armour, and how they raided across Europe and even reached America.

The Vikings lived over 1,000 years ago, but they left many traces behind, across a huge area. This means that the story of the Vikings can be assembled like a jigsaw puzzle, using these many sources. The pieces in the jigsaw puzzle are archaeological objects, such as remains of tools, weapons, skeletons, graves, buildings and towns dug out of the ground. These things can tell us how the people of the Viking Age lived – their burial practices, the weapons they used, building materials and building types, but not anything about their thoughts or feelings. For those we need written or pictorial sources, and we must distinguish between those written about them and the sources they wrote themselves.

The best sources are those the Vikings created themselves: poems, texts or pictures on runestones and other artifacts.

Some very important sources for the Viking Age are the stories preserved in Iceland, which we call sagas. The most famous are the sagas of the Norwegian kings that the Icelandic historian and chieftain Snorri Sturluson (1179–1241) wrote down in the 13th century. They take the readers on voyages of trade, plunder and conquest around the known world. There are bloody battles and exciting events, and we can hear their voices speak to us. But since Snorri lived 200 years after the events, he did not experience what he wrote about. He himself states in his book that his narratives are based on old written and oral stories and on skaldic poetry. Therefore, it is uncertain if anything he writes is true. When a historian tries to assemble the puzzle about the Vikings and would like to use the sagas as a source, he or she must ask a number of questions. Are there other sources that say the same as Snorri? It is great if there is, but then we also have to figure out which one is the oldest. This is how we dig as far back as possible. We must also ask ourselves why Snorri wrote these stories? For example, Snorri was in the service of the Norwegian king Håkon Håkonsson when he wrote about Håkon's predecessors. Perhaps he wrote them on behalf of the king? Perhaps he added to or embellished the historic facts to please Håkon?

The best thing is if when archaeological sources match the story. In 1996, archaeologists found a magnificent 36-metre Viking ship in Roskilde, Denmark. Using modern technology, including dendrochronology, it was determined that the ship was built in Vestfold in Norway in around 1025–26. In the *Saga of King Olav the Holy*, Snorri describes how Olav built such a big ship in Vestfold in 1026. It's impossible to say whether it is the same ship, but at least now we know that big ships like that were built in Norway at the time of Snorri's stories. One part of Snorri and the other sagas that is seen as a valid source is the skaldic poetry that accompanies the narratives. A vast array of Norse poetry dealing with events ranging from the migration period and up to the medieval times exists. The poetry is considered to be a genuine source because of its complexity. It had to be recited correctly not to lose its meaning. Most of the poetry is made as homage to kings and chieftains – it says less about daily life, but a lot about attitude and values.

The most important written sources are not Scandinavian at all. In addition to the large body of Norse literature we have written sources in English, Irish, French, Russian, Byzantine and Arabic. These are often contemporary, and contain eyewitness accounts. Some references are just short notes in yearly chronicles of monasteries and churches, while others are vivid accounts of customs and traditions written down by travellers. Together all these pieces reveal the complex and fascinating society of the Vikings.

Illustration by Christian Krogh of Snorri for the 1899 edition of Heimskringla, *published by J.M. Stenersen & Co. CC-BY-SA*

700–750   First use of sail in Scandinavia, enabling voyages across open sea. Increased iron production means more extensive manufacturing of weapons and tools.

780–790   Vikings establish themselves in the North Sea Islands, and begin raiding the coast of England and Scotland.

789   Vikings land at Portland and kill the king's bailiff.

793   Vikings attack the Holy Island of Lindisfarne, the centre of English Christendom.

795   Ireland and Spain targeted by Vikings for the first time.

799   The monastery on Noirmoutier in Aquitaine in France is attacked.

800   Vikings conduct trade with the tribes in Russia.

808–810   Danish king Godfred lauches several attacks on the French.

834   Two women are buried in the Oseberg ship burial in Vestfold, Norway.

835   First Vikings arrive in Byzantium.

845   Viking chieftain Ragnar attacks Hamburg and Paris.

865   The Great Heathen Army arrives in England for the first time.

866   York becomes the first Viking kingdom in England.

872   King Harald Fairhair unites western Norway under his rule after the Battle of Hjørungavåg.

879   The Danelaw established in eastern England.

880   Kiev is conquered by the Vikings and becomes the centre for the Rus-Vikings. Ohthere the seafarer from Hålogaland visits the court of Alfred the Great.

910	Warrior and poet Egil Skallagrimsson born in Iceland.
911	Viking chieftain Rollo (Rolf) establishes Normandy in France.
922	Arab traveller Ibn Fadlan meets Vikings on the Volga and describes their strange customs.
952	Eric Bloodaxe becomes the last Viking king in York.
975	Danish king Harald Bluetooth converts to Christianity under threat of invasion from Emperor Otto II.
980	Vikings become mercenaries for the emperors of the eastern Roman empire.
991	Olav Tryggvason is victorious at the Battle of Maldon, and extorts the first Danegeld from Ethelred the Unready.
1000	Leif Ericsson reaches the eastern coast of Canada, and establishes a trading outpost in America. Iceland adopts Christianity at the Althing.
1002	King Ethelred orders genocide of Scandinavian settlers in England in what has become known as the St. Brice's Day Massacre.
1014	The Vikings of Dublin lose the Battle of Clontarf, spelling the beginning of the end of Viking rule in Ireland. In England the Danish king, Svein Forkbeard, deposes Ethelred.
1016	Canute the Great becomes king of England and Denmark.
1024	Olav the Holy establishes Norway as a Christian kingdom.
1036	Sigtrygg Silkbeard expelled from Dublin after 47 years as king.
1030	Olav the Holy is killed at the Battle of Stiklestad, and Canute the Great becomes king of Norway.

1041	The imperial Varangian (Viking) guard is established in Byzantium.
1042	Harthacnut, the last Anglo-Danish king, dies and Edward the Confessor becomes king of England. The Norwegian king Magnus the Good unites Denmark and Norway under his rule.
1066	Edward the Confessor dies and the Norwegian king Harald Hardrada is killed at the Battle of Stamford Bridge by Harold Godwinson's forces. William the Conqueror then defeats Harold Godwinson at Hastings to become the first Norman king in England.
1070	Completion of the 70-metre-long Bayeux Tapestry, which recounts the Norman Conquest.
1085	Last attempt from the Vikings to re-conquer England fails.
1095	Death of Godred Crovan, the last Norse king in Dublin.
1100	The Icelandic historian Sæmund Frode starts writing down the history of the Norwegian kings.
1103	'The last Viking', Norwegian king Magnus Barelegs, is killed in Ireland in an final attempt to re-establish Norse control in the region.

THE WORLD OF THE VIKINGS 750–1100

The Vikings' homeland

Colonisation and farming

Regular plundering and imposition of taxes

→ Raids and voyages

0   500 km

0   200 miles

GREENLAND

ICELAND

Thingvellir

The Eastern
Settlement

c. 980

c. 1000

To America

The Atlantic Ocean

Faeroe Islands

The North Sea

c. 870

c. 760

Shetland

Orkney Islands

Hebrides

SCOTLAND

794

792
Lindisfarne

IRELAND

Dublin

Man

York

London

789

Bretagne

The Seine

Paris

Loire

799

Nantes

FRANKISH EMPIRE

Coruña

Pamplona

Arles

845

Luna

Rome

ITALY

PORTUGAL

SPAIN

Lisbon

Tagus

CALIPHATE OF CORDOBA

Sevilla

Balearics

Sicily

844

MOROCCO

Mazimma

Borg

Hålogaland

Lade
Trøndelag

NORWAY

SWEDE

Uppsala

Vestfold

Kaupang

Bir

DENMARK

Ribe

Hedeby

Friesland

Hamburg

Dorestad

The Rhine

The Elbe

789

Po

ILLUSTRERT HISTORIE

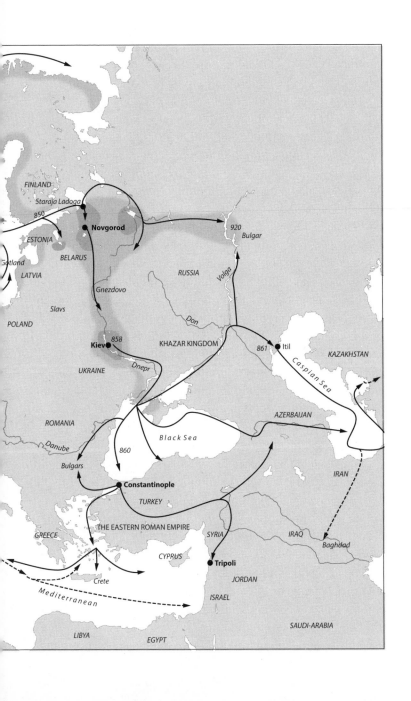

CHAPTER 1

VIKING SOCIETY

At the beginning of the Viking age a more or less homogeneous population inhabited the areas from southern Denmark to as far north as Troms in Norway and eastward to the Baltic coast of Sweden. The territory was divided into a range of smaller kingdoms, lands, counties and legal districts.

The most prosperous area, economically and population-wise, was the realm of the Danish kings. The most important reason for the kings' power was that they could control trade between the Baltic region and western Europe. From time to time the Danes also controlled the regions on both sides of the Oslo Fjord, from Agder, Vestfold and the Oslo area in Norway, southwards into modern-day Sweden to the mouth of the River Göta where the city of Gothenburg now stands. To the south, the River Eider in today's Germany formed a natural border between the kingdoms on the continent and those on the Danish peninsula. The great forests in Schleswig and Holstein also made an effective barrier towards the south. To the east, the forests and marshes in what is today Småland separated the Danish territory of Skåne from the people of Götaland.

In the Viking Age Sweden consisted of two 'peoples', the Svea and a Gothic tribe known as the Geats. These two peoples were physically separated from each other by big lakes and forests which formed a natural boundary. The Svea lived along the east coast of Sweden and in the region around Lake Mälaren. The islands of Öland and Gotland also belonged to the Svea. Estland (modern Estonia) and parts of modern Finland on the other side of the Baltic also came under the influence of the Svea. The Geats dwelt on the large plains of southern Sweden. Götaland was divided into two large regions, East Götland and West Götland.

In Norway the main population areas were in the eastern part and in the areas around the Trondheim Fjord, where agriculture was possible on a larger scale. On the west coast, the populations lived on small strips of land along the coast and fjords. The mountain areas inland were mostly uninhabited. In the northern parts of Norway the Norse population also lived along the coast. In most areas of central and northern Norway the Norse population co-existed with the Sami people, who they taxed for goods like fur, downs and walrus hide and tusks. At the end of the Viking Age, around AD 1000, the total population of Scandinavia (both free and slave) was around 1.2 million people.

Social structure

The Vikings lived in a stratified agricultural society where membership of a family, bonds of friendship and control of land were the most important determinants of status and rights. A religion largely based on war and a focus on strength and skill in combat set the framework for individual achievement. The different social layers within the population were perceived as ordained by the gods. This did not however exclude the possibility of a degree of social mobility. A person could rise to a higher social level, or sink to a lower one. Life was often a hard battle against nature and against each other.

At the top of Viking society were the kings, earls and chieftains. In the internal order of rank among these, the kings and earls sat

The word Viking was used in the Viking Age, but not as the name of a nation. There are several theories about what 'Viking' really means and its origin. It is found both on Scandinavian rune stone inscriptions and in European reports. Probably the word emerged before the Viking era as the name of a sea warrior or member of a warrior brotherhood. In the *Anglo-Saxon Chronicle*, Viking means 'pirates' or 'robbers', and as such, it was negatively charged. This is also how it is used in the sagas. Today it has become more neutral in meaning and also refers to peaceful traders and settlers from Scandinavia.

In England, the Vikings were called *Dani* or *Northmen*. In the east they were known as *Rus* and *Varjager*, and in Spain they were called *al-Madjus* – fire worshippers – meaning they were gentiles. No distinction was made between Norwegians, Swedes and Danes such as we have today. The term Viking covers the Norse (Norwegians), Danes, Swedes, Rus (Russian Vikings), Anglo-Danes, Anglo-Norse, Hiberno-Norse, Icelanders and Greenlanders.

highest and the chieftains were lowest. Chieftains could advance to become earls and even further to become kings if their family relationships allowed. This group were the absolute rulers of society, and they were admired and credited with qualities, which others did not have. Those who could claim princely or divine kinship were considered to have a number of inborn qualities. Unusually high intelligence was one such quality. They were also considered to be better qualified to lead religious ceremonies. But only a few could stand on top.

In the year 1020 a young man named Asbjørn lived at the farm site of Trondenes in Troms, in the far north of Norway. He was one of the best-liked chiefs in the north because he held great feasts several times a year where he shared a large amount of food, drink and gifts. One year, when the crops failed, he was forced to buy grain and other foods. However, Asbjørn had no plans to end the feasts, as it would mean loss of honour and status. In the end, he saw no other way but to travel to the south and buy grain from his uncle, the great farmer and chieftain Erling Skjalgsson, who was almost as powerful as the king himself. Asbjørn brought twenty men and went in a big cargo ship. At Karmøy Asbjørn was stopped by Tore Sel. Tore was a man of low status who had been granted power over the area by King Olav the Holy. He told Asbjørn that the king did not want people down south to sell their grain. But Asbjørn defied the king and bought grain anyway. On his way back he was again stopped by Tore Sel, who confiscated all the grain and goods. Asbjørn did not manage to hold any feasts that winter, and many whispered and laughed at him behind his back. This was a shame Asbjørn could not live with. The following year he went south with a warship to seek out Tore Sel and take his revenge. When Asbjørn came to Tore, both King Olav and Skjalg, the son of Erling Skjalgsson, were there to celebrate Easter. Tore bragged to the king and the onlookers how he had taken grain and equipment from Asbjørn. Then Asbjørn drew his sword and struck Tore Sel so he fell dead in front of the king. Asbjørn was arrested and King Olav wanted to kill him for what he had done. But Skjalg asked the king to wait to kill Asbjørn until after the Easter holy season was over. By then Asbjørn's uncle arrived with more than 1,000 warriors and forced the king to let Asbjørn go free. Asbjørn received a lot of praise for his revenge killing and was given the surname *Selsbane* – which means 'Killer of Sel'. But the result was that a war broke out between King Olav and Erling Skjalgsson, which led to Erling's death. Also the king's men later killed Asbjørn. Finally, Asbjørn's cousin, Tore Hund, killed King Olav at the

Battle of Stiklestad as revenge for the assassination of Asbjørn, thus changing the history of Norway.

The struggle for power between the mightiest men of the Viking era, the kings and the chieftains was fierce. The chiefs who lost such power struggles often lost all support, were killed or had to escape abroad with their warriors in order to gain new wealth to fight again.

Under the rulers and kings were the free farmers. The farmers and the chiefs supported and helped each other. For example, a chief could help a farmer with food in bad times or protect him from other rulers and robbers. The farmer had to support his chief when he asked for it. For instance, they were important participants and supporters of the chiefs in parliamentary assemblies at the *things*, and it was from the ranks of the farmers that young men were recruited into the chiefs' armies of followers. The farmers grew all types of produce, but corn and cattle were especially important. Between ploughing and harvest times, farmers who had the means and opportunity could themselves organise voyages of plunder and/or trade. There were both rich and poor farmers. The farmer who had the highest rank was called a *hauld*. His family had lived in a farm for six generations or more and he could own many large estates. Asbjørn's uncle, Erling Skjalgsson, was both a *hauld* and a chieftain, and had many servants and slaves on his farms. However, most of the farmers owned smaller farms, which they worked themselves with help from slaves and family members. The farmers were responsible for protecting those who lived on the farm.

At the bottom of the social ladder were the slaves. They were seen as real estate, similar to domestic animals. The Vikings captured a significant number of people whom they sold as slaves, both at home and abroad. There was a very long tradition of slave ownership in Scandinavia, and by the Viking Age it was a well-developed institution of great importance to the community. Somewhere between 20 and 30 per cent of the population of Scandinavia in the Viking Age were slaves. To hold them in check,

A Norse knight from the 12th century representing the elite of Norse society at the end of the Viking Age. From the Baldishol Church tapestry.

society developed a system of very harsh punishments for rebellion. Most of the small farmers did not have slaves to work their land. A medium-sized farm might have up to three slaves, and bigger farms could have many more. They did most of the heavy work. Many treated their slaves well, became friends with them and gave them enough food and protected them. A slave could win his freedom by being loyal, a good friend or by defending his master. Freed slaves formed a class between freemen and slaves, with strictly defined rights and strong obligations towards whoever had granted them freedom. Many farms made use of freed slaves and their descendants, and of landless peasants without political rights. Slaves and freed slaves could in extreme circumstances be armed to take part in the protection of their owner's or liberator's home and possessions. It could take between two and four generations before the descendants of freed slaves were counted as freemen.

Marking time

In the Viking age, individual years were not fixed as they are today. People used a relative chronology, with reference to so-and-so many years after important events, for example, 'four winters after Håkon became king'. The year was divided into two equally long periods, summer and winter, and a man's age was counted in number of winters. October 14 was the first day of the winter season, with *Gormánuður*, the month of slaughter, being the first winter month. April 14 begins the *harpamonth* and marks the beginning of summer. The year was again divided into moon phases – from new moon to new moon or from full moon to full moon. According to some sources, the Danes sometimes added a month – *the late month* – so that some years had 13 months instead of 12.

Remnants of the Viking week can be found in the names of the days of the week. Emperor Constantine introduced the seven-day week in AD 321, and Germanic tribes adopted the concept. Many of the names they gave the traditional Roman days are still in use, and show a clear connection between Roman and Norse gods: Sunday is the day of the sun, Monday is the moon's day, Tuesday is Tyr's day, or *Martis dies* (Mars's day); Wednesday (*onsdag*) is Odin's day, corresponding to the Roman *Mercurii dies* (Mercury's day). Thursday is Thor's day, or *Jovis dies* (Jupiter's day). This was the last day of the week in the Viking Age. *Blots* (sacrifices) were normally held on this day and the law assembly opened on a Thursday. The first day of the Viking week was Friday. This was Frigg's/Freya's day, in the Roman empire called *Veneris dies* (Venus' day). Saturday (*lørdag*) was bath day (*laugardag*), while the Romans called it *Saturni dies* (Saturn's day).

Instead of dividing the day into hours, the Vikings determined the time after the sun's position. The 'sun ring' (24h) was divided into eight equal parts that marked the sun's position in the sky relative to the farm. Each of these times was called a 'day mark' and had its own name. One spot was marked in the terrain where the position of the sun correlated to the position of the 'sun ring', and most people used this to tell the time. The main daymark was noon (midday). That is, when the sun stood in the south, corresponding to the point when the sun is highest in the sky and the time is noon.

Gender roles

At first glance, gender roles in the Viking Age seem clear and distinct. Men and women each relate to their own symbolic world with its rights, values and attributes. A free man had weapons as his symbol; with these he would defend himself, his kin and his property. The woman had the keys to the farm as her main symbol. Another symbolic distinction was dress and appearance, signalling both status and gender. The ideal was that the free landowner should be well-dressed and well-groomed, with hair and beard cut, while the woman should be well-dressed and have pale, almost white skin. The import and purchase of beautiful clothes and fabrics, weapons and jewellery were important prerequisites for living up to the ideals.

An Icelandic law stipulated that women who dressed like men and cut their hair or carried weapons could be outlawed. The same applied for men who wore women's clothes. However, gender and gender roles can be perceived as two different things in the Viking era. Symbols usually associated with specific gender roles are found in the context of both sexes, such as keys, weapons and jewellery. This means that a traditional stereotyped view of gender may not have been applicable in all areas of the Viking Age life; there was room for variation.

There was a clear connection between women and power in the Viking age. Not only did women exercise power within the farm collective, they also exercised power in the context of religious rituals. They formed an important link in the communication between this world and the spiritual world. Women also held important social positions and were both local leaders and rulers of larger societies. They were poets, healers, skilled craftsmen and contractors with their own ships. They led expeditions and committed trade. It is now clear that more women than previously believed accompanied the men on raids in the early stages of the Viking Age. Women played an important role as participants in the expeditions and as settlers in the conquered

Silver ornament with female figure serving drink from the 10th century, from Köping on Öland, Sweden. National Museum of Denmark. CC-BY-CA

Viking weddings

Viking weddings were traditionally held in late summer after the fields had been harvested and sufficient beer and honey mead had been brewed for the wedding party. They were usually held outdoors, and always on a Friday or 'Friggs-day', to honour the goddess of marriage. Both the bride and groom were washed and groomed and given new beautiful clothes. Then they went to a holy grove where there was an altar to the gods. The ceremony was led by a *gode*, a kind of priest, often the farmer himself. He began with sacrificial animals to the gods; a goat to Thor, a sheep to Freya, and a wild boar or a horse to Frey. The meat was cooked and eaten at the party afterwards. The priest poured the blood of the sacrificial animals into a bowl, and with a broom he sprinkled it over the altar, the couple and the guests so that they all became red with blood. Both the groom and the bride brought a sword to the ceremony. The man's sword was often a family sword carried by one of his ancestors. This was given to the woman for safekeeping and to make sure that it passed on to their son. The bride gave the groom a sword to signal that he now assumed her father's role as her protector. After the sword ritual, they gave each other finger rings that would symbolise an unbreakable bond between them. Then they were married. After the ceremony, the 'bridal run' followed, where the bride, groom and all the guests ran or rode to the longhouse where the couple would live. The bride had to be helped over the raised doorstep without falling, which would be a bad sign. The door represented the transition to her new life as a housewife. Once inside the hall, the groom threw his sword as hard he could into one of the roof posts. The deeper the sword went, the better life would be. After this, the party could begin.

areas of the mid-800s. Women also had personal honour, their actions (negative and positive) were reflected in the honour of their male relatives. A man's loss of honour also affected his wife, but unlike women in many other societies, Viking women had some control over their honour. For example, they could divorce a husband who did not respect their honour, or assume roles that were initially reserved for close male relatives, such as taking responsibility for their own wealth and making decisions about marriage, if the circumstances warranted. There are also many examples of women buried with swords and shields and other weapons. This could be interpreted as an indication that the weapons were used by the women and that therefore some women were also warriors. It is possible that women belonging to the growing class of freemen who did not own land, and therefore engaged in warfare and trade instead, could take up arms and join the men as warriors. Although the scarce sources indicate that it must have only applied to a few.

For the women in the landowning class, such alternative lifestyles must have been more difficult to achieve. They were more likely to be subject to traditional gender roles and honour codes in society. For the landowning class, the union of marriage between a man and a woman must have been one of the most important social institutions. It meant a union of two families and perhaps whole societies. It muted and ended conflicts and led to alliances, cooperation and prosperity for many. It was also an institution that ensured that land and wealth were transferred to the next generation, and – most importantly – that the family line was secured. Such a symbolic act therefore concerned the whole family, and a man had to consult with his friends and relatives before he could choose a bride. Although the law did not require a woman to consent to marriage, it seems to have been traditionally considered an important factor. Marriage should also work well. In the sagas, marriage against a woman's will always ended with tragedy, death and divorce. Big values were in play, and good cooperation between spouses must have been important. Women within the aristocratic classes, however, differed from farming-class women in that they were largely pawns in the game of politics.

Government and law

At the start of the Viking Age the whole of Scandinavia was a patchwork of numerous small kingdoms and lands ruled by minor kings and chieftains. Increasing concentration of power gradually enabled stronger kingdoms to absorb smaller ones in a steady process of nation building. The term 'land' occurred when smaller settlements grew together or were put together under a shared legal system or for shared religious practices.

All political power was based on the principle of generosity and reciprocity. The princes distributed their wealth by gift-giving and other means and gained support in return, thus forming alliances and political unions both with local farmers, and other rulers. From a political point of view, the most important 'gift' was a great feast with food and drink, provided by the prince for his supporters. Other types of gifts were protection, weapons, gold, silver, clothes, land and access to lucrative military service. Such gifts obliged the recipient to give the donor political or military support, preferably both, and thus forged a bond of friendship. If the prince broke his obligations to provide a feast or gifts, or if he was unable to hold a feast on a large enough

A Viking feast as depicted on a Gotland picture stone. Photo: Kim Hjardar

scale, the bond of friendship was broken. His supporters were then no longer obliged to maintain their bonds of loyalty but could support other princely candidates, who were seeking to strengthen their position by giving gifts and feasts. In many cases friendship, not family, was the most important social cement in the Viking Age.

The thing

During the Viking era, many settlements and parts of the country had their own laws, which were upheld at the *thing*. A thing was a legislative assembly where free men within a defined area were entitled and obligated to attend. The system of things was common throughout the Nordic region and in many of the areas where Vikings settled. There could be local things, regional things or national things. Here, free farmers, chiefs and kings would discuss common affairs, and pass judgement on cases brought forward for settlement. In many cases, money fines could settle disputes. Kings were hailed at the thing; war councils held, agreements on warfare and alliances forged, and warriors recruited. However, the things were not totally democratic – the chiefs and kings were in charge, and could get the verdicts they wanted. The farmers put their honour and life at risk if they did not support their leaders. Also, farmers had to put forward their weapons for inspection at the thing.

If someone was guilty of a crime like murder or robbery, it was the king's or chief's task to catch the criminal and bring him to the thing to be judged. If two people had a disagreement, they could also put their cases forward on the thing.

A man called the Lawsayer opened the thing assembly by reciting the laws, so that everyone could hear what law was applicable. At this time, the laws were not written down, so the Lawsayer had to remember them by heart. Twelve chosen men were picked to decide who was in the right and if the criminals were to be judged. If the accused was found guilty, he had to pay a fine or he could be sentenced to be an outlaw. An outlaw could be killed by anyone.

If the dispute could not be settled at the thing, or if the offence was such that one person felt their honour had been offended or that they had been insulted in other ways, men could settle their grievances by prescribed forms of duelling. The Icelander Egil Skallagrimsson (c. 910–990) once called a man named Atle before the Gulathing. He wanted the judges to resolve a case where Egil's wife, Asgerd Bjørnsdottir was cheated out of her father's inheritance. First, Egil talked to the judges, and made his claim about the inheritance. Egil thought that the king had unlawfully given Asgerd's inheritance to a man called Atle. But Atle denied that he had anything belonging to Egil's wife. Atle also brought many armed men with him to the thing, who all swore that what he said was true. If a rich person or a chief was accused, he could buy support from the judges. He could also bring armed men, thus making sure he was not convicted.

Egil became so angry that he challenged Atle to a duel. The old laws said that if you failed to reach an agreement on the thing, the two parties could meet for a duel called *holm-going*. Initially, the combatants met on an island (a holme) – this defined the combat area, so that noone could escape. Later on a duel would be held on land, within set boundaries. Egil and Atle both had swords and shields and they fought until Atle was killed. It was not always the case that someone had to die, and sometimes the issue was resolved when one party was wounded. Since Atle died, Egil could take all that he claimed from Atle's estate.

Many cases were resolved by duel, and some cases could only be resolved by duel. Slander and gossip or a word of abuse demanded a challenge to a duel. It was socially unacceptable not to follow up a verbal insult with weapons if necessary. If the originator of the insult failed to respond to the challenge to fight he was considered an unmanly, false and unreliable coward. The punishment was to become outlawed, which meant that anybody could take your life without having to pay a fine. If the offended party declined to fight, the penalty was less severe, but he had lost the trust of society and could no longer speak at the thing or swear an oath. If it came to a duel and the originator of the insult won, the insult was deemed to have been justified. If the offended party won, the insult was deemed unjustified and was withdrawn. In most, if not all, cases, the loser was also liable to pay economic compensation to the winner.

Such a system meant that many people were easy targets for men who were good at fighting, and there are many stories of men

Thingvellir was the main assembly site on Iceland. CC-BY-SA

Fines and punishments

It could be very expensive to kill or injure someone during the Viking Age, as the whole family could be held responsible for paying the fine. If someone was unlawfully killed, the family would have to pay silver equivalent to the sum of up to 198 cows to the victim's family. One cow may be worth as much as £1,800 pounds in today's money, so the price for murder would amount to approx £356,400. If you only hurt someone, the fine would be reduced accordingly. An index finger was valued at £5,793 in today's money, whereas depriving someone of their little finger was set at a fine of £1,448.

who earned themselves enormous wealth by travelling round and challenging others to duels. Having the law on your side counted for little if you could not defend your honour with weapons.

Growing up Viking

Children were important to the parents and the community, but they were viewed as unfinished people, without the power and strength of a responsible adult. Childhood was therefore not a highly-regarded time of life, it was just a stage on the road to adulthood.

Boys and girls did not choose their own path. As a rule, the girls in a freeholder's family would work on the farm and take care of the household, while the boy would eventually be responsible for everything that went on outside the farm. The children were raised and educated on a farm, either by their parents or by foster parents, where they could receive special education and useful skills. Many children were used as pawns in political games, and often raised far from their close family.

Children born in the Viking Age had to be healthy to have a chance at survival. There were no educated midwives and doctors, and many were born in the winter when it was cold and dark. It was the father who decided if a child would have the chance to grow up or if it was to be killed – no child was automatically a member of a family and deserving of its protection until its father had recognised it. Recognition required a solemn ceremony when the father presented the child to the gods and the people of the farm, declared that it was his child, put it on his lap and gave it his name. Only then did the child become part of the genus. Children who were not recognised were given a short life as slaves or left in the woods to die. Many children, even in rich families, died young even though they were recognised. Nor was it expected that all children would live – the people of the Viking Age lived much closer to death than we do. Death was something more natural.

In the year 850 a group of landless Vikings camped at one of the great rivers that flow through today's Russia. Among them was an Arab as their guest. He later wrote an account of his meeting. One day there was great tension in the camp, one of the men was an expectant father, waiting for news of the birth. The women in the camp walked back and forth between the tent and the fire where kettles of water boiled, while the men waited with grim faces around the fire. After a while, the message came – a boy was born! The Vikings roared loudly and hit their shields with their weapons. Then one of the older women came out carrying the boy. She lay the boy down naked on a sheepskin in front of his father and went away. The father looked at the boy and examined him carefully. Then he pulled his sword from the sheath, threw it on the ground in front of the boy and said loudly so the whole assembly could heard it: 'I do not leave you any property, you only have what you can take with this sword.' Then he put the boy on his lap and gave him his name.

This story offers a unique glimpse into the landless Vikings' view of life – you have to take what you need by the point of a sword. If the child survived his first years he would be raised to trust and use his weapon with skill. It was therefore extremely important that he learned to use it from a young age. The child's father could be absent for long periods, or he might die young. It was therefore the mother's duty to ensure that the child received the training he needed.

In the year 917, Egil Skallagrimsson was a seven-year-old boy in Iceland. He already participated in a game called 'knattleik' – a kind of ball game with clubs. Egil was younger than the other boys but he was strong. One day Egil played with a boy named Grim who was ten or eleven years old and also a strong boy. During the play Egil became angry and hit Grim with the club. Grim responded by wrestling Egil to the ground and beating him up. Egil told his cousin Tord what had happened and was promised help. Tord gave him an axe, and then they returned to the boys who were still playing. Egil ran out on the field and put his axe in Grim's head so hard that it stuck in the brain. Then they left and

A wooden play horse from the Faeroe Islands. CC-BY-CA

A wooden Viking sword found in Staraja Ladoga (Russia). CC-BY-CA

went home. When Egil came home, his father, Skallagrim, cared little about this. But his mother said that Egil seemed to be a promising Viking, and she thought that Egil should get a warship as soon as he was old enough, so he could go Viking. Egil's childhood was short, as it was for most children at the time. He was sent out on plundering raids when he was twelve years old.

Egil's story was probably not a very common one, but it illustrates the need for kids to be tough. When a boy was between ten and twelve years old, he should be able to participate in sports and travel with adults, and when he turned fifteen, he was considered an adult and was able to own property. Then he had personal responsibility and duties. He could have tasks in public life, marry, and had to participate in defence, revenge and warfare. It was expected that young boys would gain honourable reputation by participating in voyages of trade and war and travel abroad before taking over or supervising labour on the farm. The elite had similar

Picture stone from Gotland. Top half showing two men, possibly teaching a young boy how to fight. Bottom: a voyage on a ship. Photo: Christer Åhlin, The Swedish History Museum.

obligations. Like Egil, the Norwegian king's son, Olav the Holy, was only twelve years old when he was sent on such a journey. Then, according to the saga about him, he went to visit the people who lived in the countries around Norway. Olav's fleet also sailed to Finland and Russia to pick up goods like skins, honey and amber.

They also went on a pirate hunt looking for pirate ships they could rob. It was dangerous and those on board had to be well trained. When the boys returned from such a trip, they received honour and were counted as adults. Those who did not go out on such journeys were often considered a little cowardly and untrustworthy – they had not tested themselves and had no honour. It would be best to get out, if you did not want to be bullied.

The young farm girl had no such transitional period, she went straight from her childhood home into marriage. Nevertheless, there were expectations of her as a housewife. She should be able to sew and weave, bake and brew, and administer a home, and she would have received suitable training in her childhood home. It could be quite tough to be a girl in the Viking Age. In the year 1040 a heartbroken mother raised a three-meter high memorial stone for her daughter Astrid, who had died before she got married. On this stone, runes declare that she was the best embroiderer in all of Hadeland, a region north of Oslo.

If Astrid had been a regular farmer's daughter, she would have risen early in the morning from the time she was old enough to help out. She would probably have fed the animals, and then helped the other women, collecting firewood and making a fire for cooking and for warmth. After eating some flatbread at *åbit*, as the first meal of the day was called, there was washing and scrubbing of benches and tables to be done. The floors in the houses were made of hard-packed soil and these had to be swept, and all the dirt and leftovers from humans and animals had to be removed. Afterwards, Astrid had to help make a fire under big iron kettles and prepare breakfast. Then she served thick, lumpy porridge to all the workmen and got a little bit to eat herself before she went to the stream, lake or sea to wash clothes, until they had to prepare *dugurden*. This was a kind of lunch that was eaten around noon. Then she had to help wash and scrub the boilers and tubs, feed the animals and then prepare for *målbit*, which was dinner in the afternoon. Perhaps Astrid got a little free time to play? When dusk came, they went inside and she was able to pick up her embroidery – Astrid and the other girls sat evening after evening throughout the year, bending over their embroidery and sewing, with only some dim tallow lights to help them see. It was important that the girls could weave, sew and embroider. The Vikings liked beautiful, colourful embroidery that told heroic stories. And they were dependent on their own skills to make their own clothes, bedding and tablecloths – there were no local shops, and markets were expensive. In addition, the girls had to make everything they would take with them when they left the farm to marry. Since the girls could be married as young as twelve, they had to learn from a very young age how to run a farm.

The Vikings were very conscious that boys and girls had to be able to different things, and one very important thing was that girls learned to cook. It took a long time to cook in the Viking Age, since everything had to be made from scratch. One had to be able to grind grain into flour, slaughter animals and pluck birds. Meat from different animals and fish had to be salted or pickled in barrels, if it was to be preserved, and that was important knowledge. The men ate most of the food that

Kitchen utensils found in the Oseberg ship burial. Photo: Eirik Irgens Johnsen, Museum of Cultural History, Oslo. CC-BY-CA

was cooked, and the girls often had to wait and make do with the remains. The girls who became good at all of this gained a reputation and a lot of honour like Astrid, who unfortunately died before she could make use of her skill as a housewife.

Parents or other important family members decided whether a boy and or a girl could get married. It was not common for them to meet enough to get to know each other before getting married. A marriage was primarily a way to connect two families together. But the boy and the girl were asked if they would agree to marry each other, because it was important that they consented, otherwise it could end with divorce. On the other hand, we hear many stories relating how a boy and girl fell in love with each other afterwards, as in the poem *Rigstula*, in which man and wife sit and stare into each other's eyes, twisting their fingers together – very much in love. Or as when Bergtora in *Njål's Saga* prefers to die with her husband rather than live on alone: '*I was given to Njål in marriage when I was young and I promised him to share his fate,*' she said. They had been very fond of each other after they got married. Indeed it was considered very dangerous for a boy to fall in love before the wedding. If a boy fell in love with a girl and tried to search her out or write love poetry for her, there was a big chance that her father or brothers would try to kill him. The god Odin had magical formulas that he used to ensnare the girls he wanted, and love poems were therefore regarded as magic that could enchant girls. Once when the Icelander Egil Skallagrimsson was travelling in Norway, the saga recounts that he helped a farmer's daughter who had been the victim of love runes. When the farmer had said no to the courtship, the boy who was in love with her tried to ensnare her with love poems. Unfortunately, he was unskilled in the use of runes and had made her sick instead. Egil, who had mastered the use of runes, destroyed the rune stick and she recovered.

It was also common for a father or brother to prevent a girl from getting married because they wanted her to work at their farm. However, the law said that a woman could marry the third suitor who had been rejected by her guardians. Thus many girls escaped fate as an unmarried house slave on their family farm. Women who were widowed or divorced could often choose themselves whom to marry.

Old age in Viking society

The Vikings seem to have perceived life as a cycle of three categories: childhood, manhood and old age. This was in addition to the fourth, taboo-laden death, the night of life.

In the Viking age it was rare to live longer than fifty years. Most died long before this, either of sickness and toil, or perhaps in war. For those who succeeded to old age, a hard and disgraceful fate awaited. When the famous Icelander Egil Skallagrimsson grew old, he became deaf and unsteady on his legs. One day he stumbled and fell to the ground. The women teased and laughed at him: 'You're done for now, Egil,' they shouted. Egil eventually became almost blind and had to crawl around in the dirt on the floor of the house while the servants kicked him and complained that he was in their way. For a Viking warrior this was the worst fate that could happen. It was a total disgrace. This is also excellently described in a poem by another once fearsome warrior called Holmgang Bersi. He was old and sick and bedridden when he and his foster son, Halldor, were left alone in the house. Halldor lay in his cradle, which toppled over. The boy fell out of the cradle onto the floor, and Bersi could not get to him. Then he said:

> Here we both lie
> In helpless plight,
> Halldor and I,
> Have no power left in us;
> Old age afflicts me,
> Youth afflicts you,
> You will get better
> But I shall get worse.

Holmgang Bersi's ditty, Laxdaela Saga, tr. by Muriel Press

The Vikings did not value people who could not contribute. When you became so old that you could not manage yourself, you lost your property, status and position in society. If times were bad and there was not enough food for all, it happened that old people were killed, so that the young people could get their food. In some places there was a dedicated mountain to push the old people off. But more often old people were taken care of and allowed to stay on the farm. They could help raise children, tell stories and share their knowledge. In other cases, we see that old people who had had important positions, such as being a *gode* or a *völva* (priest or priestess), could be kept alive for a very long time. In the Oseberg ship grave there was a very old woman suffering both from gout and a crooked back. She may have been carried around while she lived. This woman must have had an important position in life to be taken care of for so long, and it has been suggested that she might have been a *völva*.

Appearance and dress

The Vikings were similar to today's Scandinavians in appearance. Their skin was fair and the hair colour varied between blond, dark and reddish. Genetic studies show that people were mostly blonde in eastern Sweden, around the Mälar Valley, while red-haired people were found mainly in western Scandinavia, especially in Denmark. An important difference between the Vikings and people today was height. In the Viking age, boys and girls were eight to ten centimetres shorter than today. The average height was estimated at 171 cm for men, but only 158 cm for women. Much of this was due to the fact that the food they ate was not as nutritious as today. The people at that time used their bodies more than we do today and therefore had more muscle than is usual today. But at the same time, they were also marked by hard work. Osteoarthritis, fractures and dental problems were common disorders. Another difference between the Vikings and us was that men's and women's faces looked more like each other than they do today. The male

Carving of a man with a groomed beard and moustache and short hair, from Sigtuna in Sweden. Photo: The Swedish History Museum. CC-BY-CA

craniums have more feminine features and the women's craniums show somewhat more masculine features in the Viking Age.

The people of the Viking Age were very keen to embellish themselves. Many archaeological discoveries of tweezers, combs, nail sets, ear spoons and toothpicks used by the Vikings tell us that. When the Jewish traveller Ibrahim ibn Ahmed al-Tartushi

Copy of gilded oval brooches from Norway. Photo: Kim Hjardar

from Cordoba in Spain visited the Viking town of Hedeby around 1000, he observed that both men and women in the city used cosmetics that made them look younger and prettier. From the scaldic poems, and especially the Edda poem *Rigstula* (*The Song of Rig*), we know that a good and well-groomed look was the ideal for the people in the farming and upper classes. Hair and beard should be well kept. Having a beard seems almost to have been a sign of manhood. One could be called 'beardless' in the sense of a young and immature person. In adult men, beardlessness was considered a blemish.

Women often wore their hair long. It was probably put in a knot behind the head, and the knot could be adorned with

Tattoos

Today it is a common idea that many Vikings decorated their body with tattoos. In fact, we only know of one source that describes Viking tattoos. It was the Arab Ibn Fadlan who around 920 said that the Vikings were tattooed (or painted) with dark green trees and pictures, from their fingernails to the throat. Perhaps it was common to adorn the body with marks and pictograms, or maybe it was appropriate only for certain subcultures, as seems to have been the case with another type of body modification. In many skeleton findings of men both from Sweden, Gotland and England, horizontal engraved grooves have been registered on the front upper part of the incisors. It is conceivable these men may have belonged to their own occupational group, such as specialised tradesmen or warriors. Another possibility is that it was seen as decoration and fashion.

coloured ribbons woven into the hair. Women (especially married women), could also wear head coverings, for example made of linen.

Already in the late 700s, the Vikings were fashion trendsetters. The court in Northumbria in England was criticised by the ecclesiastical Alcuin of York for copying Scandinavian hair and clothing trends. In another anonymous English letter, a man advocates his brother to follow the Anglo-Saxon custom and not indulge in 'Danish fashion with shaved neck and blind eyes'. 'Blind eyes' most likely means long brows. But long hair was also fashionable in some environments and not least classes. Among the Germanic peoples, there was a notion that long hair symbolised male virility and ruling power. When Håkon, Earl of Norway defeated the Jomsvikings of the Baltic in a battle around 990, and the prisoners were to be decapitated, one of the leaders Sigurd had long and beautiful hair which he did not want to get bloody. In another, later written source, John of Wallingford (d. 1214) describes the Vikings as well-groomed heartbreakers. He notes that they, thanks to their habit of cutting their hair every day, bathing every Saturday and regularly changing clothes, were able to 'undermine the virtue of married women' and even 'seduce the daughters of nobility to become their lovers'. Several Arab sources also mention that the Vikings used to wash themselves and wear fine clothes. Ibn Fadlan describes the Vikings as 'tall like date palms, blonde and reddish', and he recounts that they washed each morning from the same bowl that a waiter bore to the men. The chief washed himself first. He watered his hair, snowed and spat in the tub before it was brought on to the next man who did the same, and so on.

In addition, the Vikings seem to have been keen to wear jewellery to emphasise status, wealth and fashion awareness. In archaeology thousands of pieces of jewellery has been recovered from the Viking Age, in all shapes and qualities, from crudely made iron fittings to pieces of gold made by professional craftsmen. Also in the written sources we find evidence of the Viking fascination with jewellery. The Arab Ibn Rustah writes that the men of the Vikings he met in the east were wearing bracelets of gold, and Ibn Fadlan says that the women among them had beads of green glass and that they had a 'box of iron, silver, copper or gold' on the chest. In this box there was a knife pendant. This box is what the archaeologists call a oval brooch, which was something almost all women carried on their dress.

The Vikings were opportunists who quickly adapted to their surroundings. Local customs and values were taken up and mixed with their own. There can therefore be big variations in how they dressed from place to place, and in the sources they seem more concerned with cleanliness in the west than they were in the east.

Farming, food production and home life

The Vikings lived in a farm-based rural society. Only a few Viking towns have been identified, and those were mainly small trading centres. Therefore, the farm was the core of the Viking culture. The farmer and his wife lived with their closest family on the farm. In addition, there were a number of other people who were not relations. A normal farm in the Viking Age might have three to four slaves, and perhaps men who worked for the farmer in return for protection. Often a Viking farmer had responsibility for the children of others until they became adults. They then got their training on his farm. These children often belonged to more powerful men than the farmer himself, and this fostering was a common way of linking two families and forging alliances. In hectic periods, like harvest time, the farmer had the help of what is known as *lauskar* or crofter. He was a freeman who did not own land himself, but worked on other people's farms to make a living. Some crofters got permanent work and lived on the farm, others only got work when the lands were to be sown or harvested or at slaughter times.

It was a very hard life for those who lost farms, or had no farms, and fell outside society. But we do see a kind of a welfare system in the sources. *Gangfolk* or wanderers regularly visited the farms. These were old, sick or disabled people who made a living wandering between farms begging. They often stayed at the farm for a while before they had to move on. If the housewife allowed it, they might sleep with the animals in the summer or even inside by the fire in the winter months. They were usually unable to help on the farm, but they could be good storytellers, and the Vikings loved good stories.

The remains of Viking farms are often found on higher ground, located to have a good view. The Viking farmer or chieftain preferred to build his farm on a hill in the landscape to show off to anyone who travelled through the area and convey their ownership of the area. At the same time they could see approaching friends or enemies from quite a distance. The part of the farm that lay outside the cultivated fields was known as the 'Outland'. The Outland was considered a little dangerous. The Vikings believed that magical creatures like goblins, spirits, elves and *jotuns* (giants) roamed the Outland. Not all of them were friendly. The area within the fences that often surrounded the farm - the 'Inland' - was safer. Here people lived together with the spirits of their ancestors. A farm therefore had to have lands with food crops, grazing for animals, burial mounds for the dead and houses for the living.

The mightiest chieftains and kings had large halls that they used for big feasts. Archaeologists have found remnants of huge postholes that held posts up to 14 meters tall. Graves have contained carpets and equipment which may have been used in the halls. There are also poems and stories describing how the halls were adorned. These sources tell us that the halls were decorated both outside and inside with carvings and fine colours. Only the richest men could have afforded such buildings.

It was common to have one or more longhouses in the yard. The three-aisled construction of the longhouse was the predominant type of building in Scandinavia from the early Bronze Age. It was generally lower and narrower than the halls, and was from ten metres up to eighty metres long. The longer the house, the more rooms it held. This multi-functional house could contain stables, kitchens, storerooms, living quarters and rooms for entertaining. In the later Viking Age a new and larger type of longhouse emerged, called the Trelleborg type, named after the place where they were first discovered. This type of longhouse was to be found mainly on the larger farms. Smaller farms usually consisted of only the main building, and one or two secondary buildings. Larger farms could contain up to seven buildings.

In front of the longhouse there was often a square surrounded by other smaller buildings, for example, a forge for the blacksmith where he could make and repair tools and weapons. Open fire was used in the forge and so they often burned down. Therefore in some places, they are found a distance away from the longhouse for safety. The sagas say that many farms had their own bathhouses and saunas. Since we know that the Scandinavian word for Saturday, *lørdag*, comes from 'laugarday', which means bathing day, this seems plausible. Farms found near or by the sea also have a boathouse where ships and equipment were stored. A house type that is often mentioned is the firehouse, where food was prepared before it was brought into the hall or the longhouse. Some houses were very small and dug deep into the ground. These are called pit-houses and here are found remains of many different forms of craft activity. They were probably also used as residence for some of the farm's people. The womenfolk who resided on some farms had such a pit-house that was called *dyngja*, where according to the sagas, men were strictly forbidden. Here the women gathered to work, and surely also to chat and gossip.

Some buildings were built of peat, some with plant materials covered with clay, some with timber, and some even with stones. Some houses have peat on the roof, others reeds and grass, while some have wooden tiles. Houses in southern Scandinavia, where the climate is better, are different from those found in western Norway and northern Norway, where the climate is wetter and colder. And the houses on Iceland and Greenland are of course even better adapted to the climate. The houses in towns look different again, but most house frames were constructed in a similar manner. No house from the Viking Age is completely preserved. Often, you can only find the remains of walls, or of the posts that held up the roof. However, the stave churches, of which some still exist today, were built quite shortly after the Viking era and were modelled on the halls of the Vikings. They used a stave construction, based on timber posts to hold the roof in place. In many longhouses, humans and domestic animals lived together. The animals lived in one part of the house, usually the part that faced the most common wind direction. Thus the animals provided some shelter from the wind and the people got some of the heat – and the smell – from them. In the part where the

Halls similar to this one (built at Borre in Vestfold) were a main symbol of power for the migthiest men in society. Photo: Klasbu, Midgard Historical Center. CC-BY-CA

people lived, there were sitting or sleeping benches along the walls covered with skin or blankets. The farmer and housewife might have a separate room or compartment where they could sleep in their own bed. Egil Skallagrimsson, who lived in Iceland, had a longhouse with several alcoves where the main family members slept. And this may have been quite common. In these alcoves there could be nice beds with carvings on the bedstools similar to those found in the Oseberg grave. The beds were much shorter than ours and it is therefore believed that the Vikings sat while sleeping. Some historians have suggested that this was because the Vikings were afraid to die lying down. If they were sitting, they could see death coming, and that was certainly important to them.

Copy of the main bed in the Oseberg burial. Photo: Kojan & Krogvold, Museum of Cultural History, Oslo. CC-BY-CA

For mealtimes and feasting, there were benches and tables along the long walls. In the middle of one long side of the main room was placed the high seat. This was where the chieftain, the king or the farmer had his seat, and then his closest friends and family sat next to him. In the middle of the longhouse there was a fireplace that gave light and warmth. Those of the lowest rank in the household sat in the corners where it was darker and maybe a little cold. A hatch in the ceiling or in the gables let out smoke.

Some Viking farms even had water in the longhouse, diverted from a nearby stream or spring. Inside the building, the watercourse was covered by a slab or planks which were lifted up to get water. But most people did not have water in their houses, and one had go to a nearby stream to get water for washing or cooking.

Agriculture and food

Good crops made the difference between poverty and despair, and wealth and power. When the sailor Ohthere (Ottar) from Hålogaland visited King Alfred the Great in England in the 880s, he said that in Norway horses were used to pull the plough. They were bigger and stronger than bulls at the time, and it was faster. The tool which the horses pulled along was an early type of plough, which did not turn over the earth, but made a furrow for the seed. The 'ard', as this plough was called, had a strong iron fitting on the tip that made it possible to break up hard turf on land that had been lying fallow. The fact that you did not turn the soil over properly meant that you could only grow crops for a certain number of seasons before you had to leave it for a while. In order to exploit the soil better, people in some cases used to dig the soil with spades rather than using the ard. This was most common in western Scandinavia and Denmark, where the terrain conditions often made digging more appropriate, but it was also done where there were bigger farms with large numbers of slaves or good access to workmen. To dig up a field required more work, but improved soil cultivation, and you could cultivate the soil every year. Spades were made of wood but often had a shoe of iron attached to the tip to prevent wear and tear.

Cereals were the main source of food, and oats and barley seem to have been the most common varieties. Barley ripens fast and is therefore well suited for Nordic conditions, while oats is more resistant to raw and humid weather. Barley was most common in Denmark, eastern and central Norway and Sweden, and northwards to the cultivation boundary, while oats was well adapted to western Norway. It was also usual to mix the cereals and grow oats and barley together, and then a farmer was better equipped for climate challenges, and did not risk losing his entire crop if things were going bad.

Both these types of cereal have a relatively poor baking capacity, and are best suited for porridge and non-yeasted bread, such as *lefse* (a thick pancake) and flatbread. This was everyday food in the Viking era. Wheat was mostly not grown in Norway, but could be found further south in Denmark and southern Sweden and on the continent. Wheat has a much better baking capacity than barley and oats. The dough gets stickier and easier to bake out. Therefore, wheat bread was considered something extra fine, and pastries of wheat were reserved for the upper class.

In addition to cereals, it was common to grow flax and hemp. These crops were well suited for the production of textiles and ropes, both essentials which one could not be without. The Vikings also grew vegetables. The sources mention peas, beans, cabbage and onions – important supplements to an otherwise monotonous diet.

Cattle also had an important role, providing not only meat, milk and hides, but also fertiliser. The Frosta Thing Law, which applied to the Trøndelag areas in central Norway, stipulates that a tenant farmer must hold at least one piece of cattle for each *sold* with seed grain. One *sold* is 97.2 litres, which is about enough for ½–1 acre of land. In addition, the tenant farmer should leave one quarter of the soil fallow and well fertilised each year to prevent soil exhaustion. The same rules may have existed in eastern Norway, while in western Norway, where the area for cultivation was smaller and spading more common, there are no such provisions.

In addition to cattle, sheep and goats were very important, providing wool, meat and milk. Also chickens and geese – producing meat, eggs and feathers – were common domestic animals. The pig, however, was not usually found on the smaller farms, and does not appear to hold a high status as a domestic animal, despite being central to Norse mythology. One reason may be that the pig needs much more nutritious food than sheep, and therefore pork was often reserved for the upper class and aristocracy. In addition, in the Edda poem *Rigstula* it is said that raising piglets was work for the slaves.

The physical size of Viking livestock was significantly smaller than today, and they yielded less meat, milk and wool. An average cow could produce 600–900 litres of milk in one year. From this, it would have been possible to produce 20–30 litres of butter in the Viking Age. By way of comparison, milk production today is closer to 6,000 litres per cow.

The *Rigstula* also gives a good description of the food eaten by different layers of society. The poor had rough bread full of lumps. In addition, they ate *sodd*, which means 'something cooked'. Maybe it was common to boil soups from leftovers, skins and (dry) bones. When Rig visited the lower class he was served food of low status.

> A loaf of bread
> did Edda bring,
> Heavy and thick
> and swollen with husks;
> Forth on the table
> she set the fare,
> And broth for the meal
> in a bowl there was.

As Rig visits the upper classes the meal he was served was much more pleasing.

> Then forth she brought
> the vessels full,
> With silver covered,
> and set before them,
> Meat all browned,
> and well-cooked birds;
> In the pitcher was wine,
> of plate were the cups,
> So drank they and talked
> till the day was gone.

The Song of Rig, The Poetic Edda, tr. by Henry Adams Bellows

In addition to coarse bread and porridge, a normal household had calves they could slaughter on special occasions. In order for a cow to give milk, it had to calve first. Not all calves would become milk cows, and therefore they could be used as food or traded. Food in the Viking era was mostly salty, sour, rancid and monotonous. Only the richest farmers and the upper class could have a thin wheat *lefse* served on white linen cloth, with fried birds, meat and sausage. They also had wine with their food. Meat eaten by the upper classes would often be game, such as moose, deer, hare, game birds and the like. On special occasions, meat from domestic animals such as pork, mutton, beef, veal and poultry was also eaten. And in very special cases horsemeat, but this was probably primarily associated with religious practice. Birds could be caught in snares and traps, but for poor people, birds were more of a commodity than food. Pork was almost food for the gods. In Valhalla they had a magic pig, Særimne, whom they slaughtered every night and served to the gods and warriors.

To preserve meat from game, sheep and pigs, it had to be salted, dried, smoked or pickled. Salt was expensive, so half-fermented and slightly salted meat was more common than fully salted. In addition, you could store dried, smoked and half-fermented fish for a long time. Of dairy products, there would be sour milk, butter, cream and different types of cheese with a longer shelf life. There were few spices available, but salt, curds, goose-grass and other herbs of different kinds would make the food less monotonous.

When the archaeologists opened the Oseberg grave in 1904, they discovered a number of different fruits and vegetables laid down in the grave. There were sour wild apples, blueberries, onions and turnips. In addition, the Vikings cultivated vegetables such as peas, cabbage and some kind of carrots.

Beer was the drink of choice for the Vikings. It was essential for feasts and religious ceremonies and was also used to pay taxes to chieftains. It was often the woman's job to make sure a farm had enough beer and mead, as she held the knowledge of brewing. While beer was an important drink, those who had access to water also drank water, but it was not always clean. Digging a well was a difficult job and demanded a lot of resource. Milk was first and foremost used to make cheese and butter, but the sources mention that you could also drink a kind of sour skimmed milk, if you did not have beer. But if you were not sick, or did not want to be accused of being a baby, you had to drink something that was fermented – and then beer was the most common choice. Children also drank a lot of beer at the time. Egil Skallagrimsson was once denied entry to a feast by his father because he was always so drunk – he was three years old. Egil went anyway and was offered beer when he arrived. When he became an adult he once took a cruel revenge when offered sour milk instead of beer – it was not considered good custom to serve sour milk to guests.

Manufacture and trade

Trade and manufacture were prerequisites for a successful political life in the Viking Age. A vast array of products were made, exported and imported throughout the period. Exercising control over the raw materials, the craftsmen and trade centres was important. The north had much to offer the realms in the south: iron, ivory from walrus, feather, hides and skins, honey and wax, to name a few. And conversely, the elite in the Nordic region wanted luxury goods from the south, such as gold, silver, slaves, glassware, weapons and wine.

Local trade and production was also important. A chieftain or important farmer could own vast areas of land, with forests, shores and lakes. The hunter, the logger, the fisherman and the smallholder all contributed to the ruler's status. The logger brought home wood for ships, buildings, furniture and so on. The farmer was responsible for livestock, which provided skins and leathers, wool and other useful goods, and grain used for bread and beer. Furs, antlers and bones were traded or made into goods or necessities for the house. Meat of all kinds was an important show of wealth. Other kinds of important raw materials could be iron ore and whale bones. Amber was also highly priced. Already in the 200s or so ships from the Mediterranean sailed into Norwegian fjords looking for lucrative commodities in exchange for Roman luxury items and weapons. In the 700s, a trade network was established in Dorestad, Friesland (in modern-day Netherlands), situated between other trading stations such as Hamwic in Wessex, Ribe in Denmark, Truso in Poland and Birka in Sweden. At the end of the 700s, new trading routes occurred. Some of the most important ports were Staraja Ladoga in Russia today and Truso in Poland. Most of the trade, though, was local.

To gain value, the raw materials needed to be processed. A skilled craftsman or -woman therefore had great value. Their products could be traded or shown off as an emblem of the ruler's status, as shown in buildings, ships, carvings, weapons, jewellery, tapestries, embellishments for clothing and so on. The members of a household needed clothing and tools. Wool and flax was spun into yarn, using a drop spindle, dyed with local or imported dyestuffs, woven into cloth and sewn into garments and household furnishings. The better made clothes, the higher status they gave.

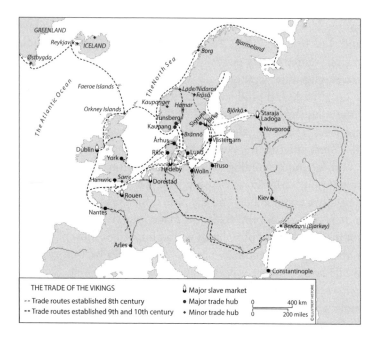

During the early 800s, the trade network experienced its peak, but in particular Dorestad was exposed to regular looting from Vikings and lost its dominant position in trade between the North Sea region and the Baltic States. Instead, Hedeby in

Viking weights, coinage and currency

In the Viking age, value was measured in silver pieces with weight. From archaeological finds we have weights made of lead, bronze or iron, often stamped with small characters. Also small folding bowl scales were found stored in round cans or boxes of bronze. The smallest unit was a 'penning', which is the same word as 'penny' today. A penny was worth about 27 pounds in today's money. There were about 30 pennies to an 'øre' (ear), which was 24.5 grammes of silver. One 'øre' was the most common measure in Viking times. For that, you could buy about 41 meters of cloth material. A cow cost about 75 pennies, and a medium good slave approx. 350 pennies (about 9,200 pounds).

1 mark = 8 øre (ear) = 24 'ertog' = 240 pennies
1 mark = 3.2 cows, 1 cow = 2000 pound
1 ear = 41 meters of vadmel (thick woollen cloth)
1.5 mark = one slave

Penny coins were first struck in Norway by Olav Tryggvason in the years 995–1000, using Anglo-Saxon coins as their model. However, in the southern Danish towns of Ribe, Hedeby and Lund, coins were minted earlier, in the first half of the 9th century. Some of the Hedeby coins were copied from the Carolingian coins of Dorestad.

A copy of a folding bowl scales from the 10th century and silver pennies and hacksilver for trade and payment. Photo: Kim Hjardar.

Denmark grew as a hub for the exchange of goods between the Baltic Sea and the North Sea. Kaupang in Norway became an important part of the Danish king's control of the trade in the Nordic region, as the point of origin for typical Norwegian goods such as iron bars, grinders and grindstones and soapstone vessels.

From the late 800s Arab silver coins called *dirham* and mass-produced glass beads and other luxury goods from the Near East flowed into the Nordic region in exchange for local goods. At the same time, there was a dramatic increase in Viking attacks at trade centres in and outside the Nordic region. Many places that acted as hubs for long-distance trade disappeared or lost significance because of these attacks. The response to this threat was that trading centres like Hedeby, Birka and Staraja Ladoga were fortified with city walls and garrisons.

The lucrative trade in Arab silver reached its peak between AD 930 and 970. Locally struck silver coins eventually took over as an important means of payment, and ship technology developed specialised merchant ships like the *knarrs*. The emergence of a more specialised trading network was the result of stronger royal powers providing protection for sea travellers. In the latter half of the 900s, cheaper raw materials such as dried fish were also important for the long-haul sailing networks. But it is important to note that only a minority of traders participated in long-distance trade. Most of the trade was of local character, where trade in food, feed, animals and local products was of primary importance.

Ships

The ship was the most important means of transport in the Viking Age and a central prerequisite for political power and prestige, which in many cases was based on the control of the sea and shipping lanes. There were many different types of Viking ship, ranging from fishing boats and cargo ships to huge warships.

The first Viking ships with sailing capacity were rigged for coastal traffic, and were either small cargo vessels (*børinger*), or a mix of warships and freight ships – *barges.* The Gokstad and the Oseberg ship are the best examples of the latter type. These types of ships were gradually improved and developed into larger and more specialised ships, the longships of the late Viking area being the most impressive.

The increased sophistication of Viking ship technology from the end of the 8th century onwards has been put forward as an important prerequisite for Viking expansion and attack. The Viking ships were slim, flexible and fast, and had shallow hulls, meaning that they could sail up shallow rivers and other waters and land on beaches out of reach of defenders. They could sail on Russian rivers down to the Black Sea area and the Byzantine empire. Surprise attacks became a major opportunity with these types of ships.

In addition, from the mid-700s, the use of sail techology gave Viking ships a wider range of operation and access to lands like the North Sea Islands, Ireland, Iceland, Greenland and North America. However, there is great uncertainty about when and where the sail was first taken into use in the Nordic region. Already in the 7th century it was probably known and used in some places, and by the mid-8th century it must have been commonplace. Gotland was an early power centre in the Baltic Sea, and the sail was probably first put into use here. Also the eastern coast of Jutland and Funen in Denmark and Karmøy in Norway, with its rich Roman Age finds and early power centralisation, may have been places where sailing began early. It made it possible for seafaring northerners to participate not only in robbery and plunder expeditions but also trade and colonisation on a completely different level than before.

More iron production from the mid-700s onwards also led to an increase in shipbuilding and weapons manufacture, which in turn made increased warfare possible. Shipbuilding on a large scale required fairly regular access to iron for tools and nails. In a ship like the Oseberg ship from the 820s there were at least 5,000 nails, forged with more than 125 kg of iron.

Excavations of several ships in Roskilde and Hedeby in Denmark have shown us that the huge warships that occur in the sagas, and in particular in the sagas of Olav Tryggvason and Olav the Holy, were not literary fantasies, but represented actual ship types, built for extensive warfare and domination. The longships occurred approximately at the same time as the specialised cargo ships, the *knarrs*, in the 10th century. They were large open boats with clinker-built hulls, usually of oak. They had strong, shallow keels, high stems, and many pairs of oars in addition to a large rectangular sail. They were, however, mainly rowed.

The most prominent symbol of the Viking longship ship is the dragonhead fixed to the post of a ship. This was often a sign of owner's kingly or chieftain status. The dragonhead could also scare off people and spirits, or mark the ship as a warship. The heads were painted in several colours, and could take the shape of intimidating dragons or snakes, and in some cases human heads.

Another characteristic feature of the warship is the use of shields along the rim. The shields signalled that the ship was a warship and were often hung outside the rim on either side of the ship,

VIKING SHIPS IN SCANDINAVIA

There are two groups of Viking ship finds from Scandinavia: burial ships and sunken ships. In total about 25 Viking ships have been discovered.

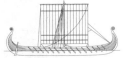

THE OSEBERG SHIP

Built: *c.* 812, Vestland, Norway
Found in burial: Vestfold, Norway
Material: Oak
Length: 21.5 m

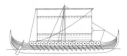

THE GOKSTAD SHIP

Built: *c.* 890
Found in burial: Vestfold, Norway
Material: Oak
Length: 23.8 m

THE TUNE SHIP

Built: *c.* 940
Found in burial: Østfold, Norway
Material: Oak
Length: 18.67 m

THE ÄSKEKÄRR SHIP

Built: *c.* 930 by Äskekärr, Sweden
Found: Alafors, by the Göta River, Sweden
Material: Oak
Length: 16 m

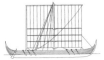

THE KLÅSTAD SHIP

Built: 998
Found: Viksfjord, Vestfold, Norway
Material: Oak and pine
Length: 21 m

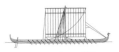

THE LADBY SHIP

Built: *c.* 900
Found in burial: Ladby on Fyn, Denmark
Material: Oak
Length: 21.5 m

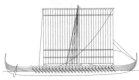

SKULDELEV 2

Built: 1042 in Ireland
Found: Skuldelev by Roskilde Fjord, Denmark
Material: Oak
Length: 30 m

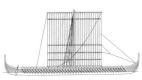

ROSKILDE 6

Built: *c.* 1025 in Vestfold, Norway
Found: Roskilde harbour, Denmark
Material: Oak
Length: 36 m

The Oseberg ship on display in Oslo. Photo: Museum of Cultural History, Oslo

attached to a list inside the rail with a rope. The shields on the Gokstad ship were about 1 meter in diameter. They overlapped each other and were painted yellow and black. It may have been the norm to also have painted hulls and colourful sails.

Leisure and sport

The Vikings were keen on competitive activity – both mental and physical – and loved winners. The word 'sport' (*idrett*) was not only used for physical activities, but could include activities such as poetry, runewriting, and pictorial arts, as well as chess and dice games and physical combat games.

The stories of the sagas indicate that most common types of games were outdoor activities, while only a few were associated with indoor activity. Outdoor activities were mostly physical games and competitions. Big tournaments involving participants and audience members from many different districts were held on special occasions, for example during the gathering of the thing, or in connection with religious ceremonies and festivals and market activity.

The main purpose of sporting activities was to teach the skills needed for real combat in a relatively harmless way. Boys started practising different sports at the age of five or six, and by the age of ten they should be able to participate in competitions with adults. When a boy was between twelve and fifteen, he was expected to be a fully fledged athlete. Combat games were exercised by men of all ages, and competition could be tough and dangerous. Egil Skallagrimsson is said to have killed his first opponent during a sporting event at the age of seven. Even though sports could be brutal, they were exercised according to certain rules and with great respect for the participants' lives and limbs. Consciously attempting to hurt anyone during a combat game was perceived as a lowly act.

A number of sports can be linked directly to the art of warfare. Some of the most important were running, stone and spear throwing, weightlifting, ball games, wrestling, archery, long jump and weapon play. In addition, knowledge of horseriding, hunting and swimming was part of the repertoire. In winter, you had other types of sports. Skiing and ice skating were common pastimes.

In the sources we also hear about some balancing exercises. This was important knowledge during combat on ships and in rough terrain. The most popular balancing game was to walk or run on the oars of a ship while it was being rowed.

The most popular individual physical sport was wrestling. In such competition a man could match himself against others and win praise and personal honour. There were two types of wrestling: regular wrestling and *Glima*. In regular wrestling the opponents had their hands around the waist of the opponent. The goal was to throw your opponent to the ground without using any tricks. In *Glima*-wrestling your right hand holds on to your opponent's belt, while your left hand and your legs can be used freely. You must then get your opponent to lose equilibrium and throw him to the ground. It was important that a warrior caught in man-to-man combat knew how to quickly bring his opponent down.

Ball games must have been the most popular type of team games, both for the participants and for the audience. A variety of ball games were played outdoors by both children and adults. These are commonly known as *knattleikr*. The rules for these types of games are not known in detail, but from the sagas it can be deduced that they involved full body contact between the players. In some games, a kind of racket or hockey stick was used to catch and hit the ball. At least four participants from each team were on the field at the same time and the opponents were placed opposite each other. *Knattleikr* was a men's sport where women, as far as we know, never participated actively. In addition to ball games, the sources mention a kind of hockey game, *sköfuleikr*. Unfortunately, the game rules are not described, except to say that the players were divided into teams and each had one selected opponent. Both games were very raw and physically exhausting and the games often resulted in the death of some of the participants, according to the sagas.

When it comes to indoor activities, poor lighting in the Viking House often restricted them, but we know from archaeological finds that the Vikings loved many types of board and dice games and gaming is also a favourite motif in the sagas and in Norse poetry. Board games often go under the common name *tafl*, meaning 'board'. The most famous Viking game is *Hnefatafl* or the 'king's table', which was played in Scandinavia as early as AD 400. Various versions are found in excavations from Ireland in the west to Ukraine in the east. The game is about a Viking king who is being attacked in his fortress, and with the help of his warriors the king will try to escape to one of the four corners. Through such games there was entertainment, competition and training of tactical skills. During the late Viking Age and the early medieval period, chess seems to have replaced the 'king's table' as a favourite board game among the Scandinavians.

One popular sport was writing and performing skaldic poetry, and those who mastered it were admired like modern pop stars. Many Viking kings were also known to play music and compose poetry, but the competition was fierce, and it became more like a professional occupation for many. Powerful kings and chiefs always had a poet or two around. They would sing about the chieftain's exploits and tell everyone how brave, generous and handsome the chieftain was.

Egil Skallagrimsson is considered one of the very best skalds of the Viking Age. One of his most famous poems is a homage poem that he made to King Eric Bloodaxe. Eric had actually planned to cut off Egil's head, but would let him keep his life if he made him a worthy poem, which he did in one night. According to tradition a chief or king had to give fulsome thanks for a honorary poem and grant the poet valuable gifts or, preferably, a gold ring. The best skalds could have their entire arm covered in gold rings. Many of their poems were remembered and recited everywhere and became hits. The skalds were serious entertainers in the halls of the Vikings, but so were also the musicians.

Norse written sources mention many different types of musical instruments. Several types of horns are known from archaeological finds. Other types of instruments may have included bells or rattles, which are usually found in graves. Some instruments may also have been made of jaw bones and are played by rubbing a wooden stick or a bone against the jaw bone.

Copies of different gaming pieces and dice. Photo: Kim Hjardar

Language and writing

Vikings spoke a language called Old Norse (*norrønt*), which evolved from proto-Norse, a Germanic language widely spoken in northern Europe. In the Viking Age, Norse evolved into the three regional dialects, western-Norse (Norwegian-Icelandic), eastern-Norse (Danish-Swedish) and the now dead language of Old-Gutnic (Gotland).

The writing system in the Viking era was *runes*; characters designed to be carved into wood, bone or metal. In a society without paper or parchment this was a good option. The runes were modelled on the Latin letters of the Roman empire, which the Germanic peoples had come into contact with at around the time of the birth of Christ. For a long time, runes and the Latin letters existed side by side. Runes were well suited to convey short private messages, while the Latin alphabet was used in official contexts. The Latin script eventually took over, mainly because it was the writing of the Church and the king. But until it gained a firm foothold in the Middle Ages, runes were still used to inscribe stone epitaphs and memorial words, magic spells, and proprietary and personal messages.

The runic alphabet is called *futhark* after the first six characters of the system. During Roman times and the migration period the runic alphabet had 24 characters, which were then reduced to 16 in the Viking Age. In the Middle Ages, the number of characters rose to 32 to adapt to the Latin alphabet. The runes continued to be in use all the way up to the 19th century in some remote parts of modern-day Sweden.

THE VIKING FUTHARK

RUNE	LETTER	NAME	MEANING
ᚠ	f	Fe	Wealth
ᚢ	u	Ur	Iron/Rain
ᚦ	þ	THurs	Jotun/Giant
ᚨ	ą	As/Oss	Aas (god)
ᚱ	r	Reidh	Ride
ᚲ	k	Kaun	Wound
ᚼ	h	Hagall	Hail
ᚾ	n	Naudhr/naud	Need/lust
ᛁ	i	Is/iss	Ice
ᛅ	a	Ar	Abundance
ᛋ	s	Sol	Sun
ᛏ	t	Tyr	Tyr (god)
ᛒ	b	Bjarkan/bjarken	Birch
ᛘ	m	Madhr/madr	Man
ᛚ	l	Logr/lög	Liquid
ᛦ	R	Yr	Yew Tree

Illustration of runes and their meaning

Music seems to have been played in everyday life, but also on various special occasions such as weddings, official celebrations, funerals or religious ceremonies. *Gange-Rolf's Saga* describes a wedding where harps, fiddles, bagpipes, drums and horns were played.

In addition to music, various types of dramatic performances were performed alongside poetry and music. These may have included miming and jester theatre. Two masks made of felt, which may have been used in a form of drama or ritual activity, have been found in the port of the then Danish trading town of Hedeby.

CHAPTER 2

A CULTURE OF COMBAT

THE PRIMARY GOAL OF WAR is to gain glory, wealth and above all, honour for the participants. Honour was what the Vikings coveted most of all, according to the sagas, the skaldic poems and the rune stone inscriptions. This saying from the poem called *Hávamál,* describes perfectly what a Viking life was all about:

> Cattle die,
> kinsmen die
> you yourself die;
> I know one thing
> which never dies:
> the judgment of a dead man's life

Hávamál is a poem in a collection of Old Norse poems from the Viking Age. It provides advice for living, proper conduct and wisdom. The verses are attributed to Odin, 'the high one' and are for the most part composed in the metre *Ljóðaháttr,* a metre associated with wisdom verse. *Hávamál* is both practical and philosophical in content. The main message of nearly all such poems is advice on how to gain, and not lose, honour in the old Norse society. They praise those who fulfilled the ideals and scorn those who do not. Honour could be obtained in several ways: through courage in battle, looting, revenge, faithfulness toward friends, family and your leader and so on. Successful military campaigns gave honour in themselves, but also provided economic power for the elite so that they could attract supporters through giving presents and hosting feasts, which in turn created glory. Gaining honour through plunder and war could thus be a good way for many young men to advance in society.

Letters and chronicles written by monks in France and England tell us that the Vikings were notorious for robbing monasteries and cities in Europe. But what is almost as impressive is that also Byzantine and Arab writers from the Middle East and Asia wrote about the Vikings' visits to distant lands like Turkey, Azerbaijan, Iran and Iraq, and foreign cities like Istanbul and Baghdad. If someone travelled so far in a sailboat or horseback through unknown lands, there must have been something that was very important for them to get hold of. A man named Ibn Miskawayh wrote down a story of such a voyage.

Once, in the autumn of 943 a Viking fleet sailed with 500 warriors on the Caspian Sea off the coast of Azerbaijan. They came from the area of modern Sweden and Norway. The fleet sailed up the river Kura until it came to the fortified town of Barda. News of the approach had preceded the fleet, and a local force of some 5,000 men, mostly farmers and volunteers, assembled on a wide plain outside the town, ready to oppose the intruders. They were uncertain who these strangers were or what they wanted, and so they allowed the Vikings to land and organise themselves. The Vikings were able to dig ditches, build barricades and organise and arm themselves before the farmers attacked them. The Vikings defended themselves well and counter-attacked. Yelling wildly, they charged forward. Overwhelmed, the conscripted peasant army fled in panic. The Vikings killed thousands of them and pursued the rest into the city itself and closed the city ports behind them. The inhabitants sued for peace and the Vikings agreed to accept the townspeople's submission and demanded everything of value in the city. This truce appeared to hold for several days, but when Muslim troops from nearby towns began to gather round Barda, the townspeople became agitated. People

Picture stone depicting scenes of raids, warfare, sacrifice and revenge. The Stora Hammars stone from Gotland. Photo: Kim Hjardar.

soon started to attack the Vikings by throwing stones at them. At the same time, the Muslim troops started to attack the town. Despite having to defend themselves on two fronts, the Vikings managed to both control the townspeople and defend the town walls. The people continued their harassment of the occupying forces, and eventually the Vikings lost patience with them. The inhabitants were given three days to leave the town, but only a few had done so when the deadline expired. The Vikings then began a wholesale slaughter of the population. Hundreds of men were killed. Women and children were herded together and packed into the town fort. Prominent citizens were assembled in the mosque and given a choice between purchasing their freedom or being killed. Many paid up, but more refused to pay and were killed. Women of all ages and the youngest boys were enslaved.

The ruler of Azerbaijan at that time was al-Marzuban ibn Mohammed. In spring 944 he personally came to Barda at the head of an army of 30,000 men to chase out the Vikings. He made several attempts to storm the city, but failed to force the walls and his troops managed to enter the city in only a few places. A small group of five Vikings were surrounded by Muslim soldiers in one of the city's gardens. The soldiers attempted to capture the Vikings, but the Vikings refused to surrender. In the end only one was left alive, a young beardless youngster, fair of face and son of one of the chieftains. But they did not manage to take him either, for when he realised that he was in danger of being taken alive he climbed a tree, stabbed himself with his knife and fell dead on the ground. The Vikings would rather die than surrender and lose honour.

Disease soon spread through the town, affecting citizens and Vikings alike. Unburied corpses spread further death in a population weakened by famine. The situation soon became so desperate that the Vikings sought peace talks with al-Marzuban. He offered them free passage if they left the town, but this was a ruse. Once the Vikings were out of the town hundreds of them were killed including the chieftain, whose name we do not know. The survivors fled back into the town to seek refuge, but disease continued to decimate them. Eventually they saw no other option but to withdraw. Under cover of night they took whatever booty they could carry, together with a number of slaves, crept back to their ships and disappeared along the river. We do not know what befell them after that. Perhaps some of them returned to Scandinavia many years later, laden with beautiful clothes of silk fabric and silver, and recounting tales of glory. Many such exotic products have been found in the graves and cities of Vikings.

From stories like this one, we learn that the Vikings went on expeditions to gain wealth and honour and that they would run great risks to get it.

Weapons of war

Weapons found buried as grave goods are the most important available material evidence of how Vikings were armed and equipped. Axes are the most usual weapons discovered in burials, but swords and spearheads are found almost as frequently. The most richly equipped graves also have arrowheads and equestrian gear. Helmets or other personal armour are hardly ever found in graves.

Free men in the Viking Age were expected to carry weapons. They had both a right and a duty to be armed, and there was a strong obligation on all men to maintain the weapons needed for the defence of the land. The laws of the Vikings required every free man to have at least three basic weapons: a spear, a shield and either a sword or an axe. Fines and punishment could apply if you had no weapons. Using and carrying weapons were natural to the Vikings. An axe was the first thing a young man learned to use. It was quite cheap and could be used as both as a tool and a weapon. A sword was a more expensive weapon, and not all young men had the means to acquire a sword, so carrying one was a mark of distinction. Those who wore swords owned

Various weapons and armour from Norwegian finds. Photo: Eirik Irgens Johnsen/Ernst Schwitters, Museum of Cultural History, Oslo

more land and had people in their service. The different types of weapons also reflected their owners' positions in society. If you were a free farmer of some standing you must have a sword, even if it was not a good sword – a lot of swords from the Viking era were cheaply made and not very practical in combat, but others were made by master smiths and decorated with both gold and silver and had names such as 'Parasite stick', 'Nailer down', Armour-biter' and 'Leg-cutter'.

The spear was the most important weapon of war. It was cheap and one could reach an enemy at distance. Everyone therefore had spears. The Vikings used round, flat, colourful shields made of wood and leather to defend themselves. They also used bows and arrows, both for war and hunting.

Weapons in mythology

Old Norse poetry and mythology can give us an idea of what the various types of weapon represented in Viking Age society. Axes and clubs are primitive weapons, used by the brutal and hot-headed. The sword, on the other hand, belongs to the mature, prosperous and just. Spear and bow are for the sharp-eyed hunter, a master at controlling himself and his weapon and focusing on wisdom (knowledge). The shield is feminine and cowardly, but necessary if you want to stay alive. Weapons are also closely connected with both mythology and the god-given classes. In the Old Norse poem *Rigstula* the four social classes are listed and set in relation to specific tools, weapons and animals. We read how the slave, who tends to the pigs, has only a knife as his tool, and no weapons. The free man (working class) controls oxen, ploughs and uses an axe. The earl rides a horse, masters the use of sword, shield, spear and bow, and owns many farms. The earl's son, the young king, is his father's superior, the wise ruler. This corresponds in turn to the realm of the gods, which were also connected to various weapons. Thor, the thunder god, has the axe or hammer 'Mjolnir' as his symbol. With this he makes order from chaos. Frey has the sword, 'Laevatein' as his. He represents the mature and cultivated farmer god. Odin, the wisest of gods, has the spear 'Gungnir' as his symbol, but also a white shield, and Freya, the giver of life, has the shield as her symbolic weapon. She is also called a Shieldmaiden.

In reality all members of the free classes used all types of weapons. Some kings actually favoured the axe and used it as their main weapon. A warrior with a two-handed axe was a fearsome and hard-hitting enemy. We hear about the axe 'Hel' when King Magnus the Good led his men to victory against an army of heathen Vends at Lyrskog Heath, north of Hedeby, in Denmark in 1043:

Ahead with his broad axe
Tirelessly forward and first,

Hordaland's king, surrounded by
A sea of swords, cast his chain-coat,
Changed earthly armour for heavenly,
Grasped the shaft with both hands;
Hel cleaves, heads fall.

Arnor Tordsson Jarlaskald, *The Saga of Magnus the Good*

Types of weapons

There are three main categories of axes; narrow-bladed, bearded and broad-bladed. The narrow-bladed axes had a blade length of 5–10 cm and were general working tools. A bearded axe had a longer edge, designed to split tree-trunks into planks and beams. Broad-bladed axes, which appeared in the second half of the 10th century, are the type most characteristic of the Viking Age. They were not bearded, but nevertheless the cutting edge could be as long as the length of the axe-head, up to 25 cm, resulting in a triangular type of shape. Broad-axes were made specifically as battle-axes. Raised high on a long, two-handed shaft, a broad-axe was a frightening and characteristic weapon of the Vikings, and probably the most famous of all Viking weapons.

Many Vikings also carried a knife to use as a weapon. There are several types known. One type of long knife was known in Old Norse as a *sax* (in Anglo-Saxon: *seax*), and another was an eastern-style knife found in the region around the Baltic, especially the Mälar Valley in eastern Sweden. These knives are mostly from the 10th century. Both types often had richly metal-ornamented sheaths and the handle is often enhanced with coils of thin silver thread at the blade end and a bronze plate with a ring at the back. The leather sheath was folded round the back of the knife, with the join along the cutting edge held together by a number of small metal fittings, with larger fittings towards the tip and the mouth of the sheath. These metal fittings include rings, for hanging from a belt.

The Viking sword was a single-handed weapon leaving the other hand free to hold a shield. Despite all its qualities and high status, the sword was a reserve weapon when it came to battles, but the weapon of choice if fighting a duel or in one-to-one combat. There are many types of Viking swords, and different types are popular in different periods. Several thousand Viking Age swords have been found in Scandinavia and beyond, which testify both to its importance as a grave good and its popularity among the living.

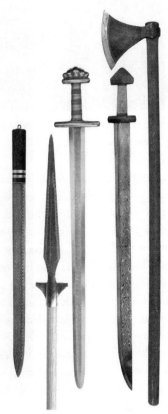

Copies of the Vikings' favourite weapons. L–R: Eastern weapons knife, winged spearhead, decorated double-edged sword, single-edged sword and a broad axe. Photo: Kim Hjardar

Viking Warrior with axe and sword on a stone cross from Weston Church in North Yorkshire. Photo: Creative Commons

A Viking sword was generally around 90–95 cm long, rarely over one metre. It could be single-edged, but two-edged was the most common. Some had inlays of twisted iron rods along the blade and some even used writing as decoration. On some the edges were only made of normal iron and thus became blunt and ridged in use, but the best had steel edges. The hilt of a Viking sword consists of three or four main parts. These are the back-hilt, the grip and the fore-hilt, with the back-hilt often consisting of two parts, of which the very hindmost is called the pommel. Unlike the other types of weapon, swords were already being decorated with precious metal from the beginning of the Viking era. Almost half of all Viking swords were decorated with silver and bronze inlay. The most richly decorated swords may have been used as much for status as for fighting.

A spear was of little monetary value compared with a sword, but nevertheless it appears to have been associated with the very highest members of society. This may be because spear and javelin were culturally connected with hunting large animals, which was a form of hunting legally reserved for the upper classes on the continent. Spear and javelin were also seen as the first among weapons because they were the longest and had the greatest range. The dominating length of the spear made it the most important weapon when armies came to close combat. A well-organised front line of spearmen had a big advantage against enemies with shorter hand weapons. The length of the spear made it not only an attack weapon but also a means of defence, able to keep opponents at a distance. The heads of smaller throwing spears were just about 20 cm long, almost as short as an arrowhead, but the strongest thrust-spears could have heads over 70 cm, well on the way to the length of a sword. Some spears have two projections on the side of the socket, known as wings. Wings originated on spears for the hunting of large animals, where the wing functioned as a barb to keep the spear in the prey and hinder a large, angry animal from coming close enough to attack the hunter. Occasionally, the back end of the shaft is capped with a metal ferrule.

Bow and arrow were clearly the Vikings' most important support weapons. A group of archers could send a heavy shower of arrows over the enemy from a range of more than 100 metres. In the Gula Thing and Frosta Thing Laws from the early Middle Ages, we read that farmers who were called up for military service should have one bow and 24 arrows per rowing thwart in the ship, i.e. one bow per two men. We can distinguish between three basic types of bow in the Viking Age: longbow; Finnish bow, made from two different woods combined; and horned bow. The Vikings generally used longbows made from a single piece of wood, preferably yew tree or elm. A longbow was nearly round or D-shaped in cross-section and the grip was an integral part of the bow. The Finnish bow, used mainly by the Sami people, was made from gluing birch and pine together, with birch as the back of the bow on the outside and pine as the belly of the bow on the inside of the arch. The composite horned bows were made from three materials; horn, wood and sinew glued

Two magnificent swords from Steinsvik in Nordland and Ånes in Hedemark, Norway. Photo: Erik Irgens Johnsen, Museum of Cultural History, Oslo

together. They can be seen as a more extreme development of the two-wood bow. They were not in widespread use in Scandinavia in Viking times. However, in the Viking town of Birka there are instances of fittings and parts of personal armour typical of the eastern tradition of mounted cavalry archers. There is no evidence of the use of crossbows in Scandinavia in Viking times.

The shield was the most basic and common defensive weapon. The Vikings appear nearly always to have used round shields. The wooden shield-plate was flat with a hole in the middle where a wooden carrying handle was mounted crossways on the inside. A dome of plate iron, the shield-boss, was nailed securely over the hole on the outside, to protect the hand. The diameter of Viking Age shields is 80–95 cm. A shield plate was made of several thin planks of wood and a layer of rawhide glued onto the whole of the front and the whole of the back to make it durable. On well-preserved finds, stitch holes can be seen round the edge of the shield, where an edging band of rawhide has been folded round and sewn securely for reinforcement. Together, these enhancements reduced the risk of the wood splitting and made even shields made of softwoods such as pine capable of stopping arrows and spears and withstanding blows from sword and axe. The shield had to be light, so pine and spruce softwoods were preferred. The Gokstad ship in Norway, dated AD 905, contained remains of several dozen shields. Analysis of these shows that most of them are made of spruce, though some may have been of pine. But also maple and yew shields have been identified in graves in Sweden.

Helmets used in the early Viking Age consisted of several iron plates nailed together. They usually had a round top, but there was a trend towards more frequent use of spike-topped helmets, eventually forged as a whole from a single piece of iron. There are only three documented finds of Viking Age helmets in Scandinavia. The most complete of these is a round-topped helmet with spectacle-shaped face protection, found in a grave near Gjermundbu in Buskerud, Norway, and dated to 950–75. This grave also includes chainmail armour made from a web of iron rings, reserved for professional warriors and the very top ranks of society. This type of armour predominates in Scandinavia, even though the archaeological finds are very few.

Helmets and mail were very expensive and confined to the upper classes and professional warriors. The nature of archaeological finds also depends largely on what the people at that time considered appropriate to use as grave goods, and the reason for their scarcity does not mean the Vikings did not use helmets and body armour, but that they were not put into graves. Perhaps their function was covered by the shield, which is nearly always present.

The other type of armour we know from Viking times was lamellar armour. This consisted of oblong iron plates, laced together with leather thongs in such a way that they overlapped, forming a flexible and partly telescopic tube round the torso. The only Scandinavian finds of lamellar armour from the Viking Age are from the trading town of Birka. The lamellae from Birka can be dated to the first half of the 10th century.

No remains of textile armour survive from the period, but Old Norse texts mention armour made of cloth, referred to as weapon shirt and gambeson. A gambeson could be made up of as many as 30 layers of cloth and be up to one cm thick. We can assume that a weapon shirt was much thinner. Linen cloth was considered particularly suitable, especially for the outer layers, but woollen felt was probably used in the middle. Much of the textile armour's strength came from parallel rows of stitches running right through all the layers to create a thick, solid, composite textile gambeson.

About a third of all the weapons used by the Vikings were imported, mainly from the Frankish empire. From the Viking Age, there are rich finds of Frankish spearheads and double-edged swords in Scandinavian graves. So many weapons were exported that the Frankish kings saw the need to ban the export of coats of mail and swords, whether by sale or as gifts. In 864 a later Frankish ruler, Charles the Bald, went so far as to introduce the death penalty for exporting weapons to the Vikings. Arab sources relate that Vikings by the River Volga in 922 carried broad-bladed swords with French decoration. Skaldic poetry also refers to weapons from France and in particular from Poitiers in western France and Rennes in Normandy. These weapons are described as having been acquired either as valuable gifts or by plunder. The skald Tjodolv told of this after he had been in the service of King Magnus the Good in the wartime year 1044:

I bore a shield home from the strife,
as my share, from Geat-land.
Strong storms with waves of swords
in the southern summer gave me mail too.
I got good weapons, a flood
before it abated.
I won a helmet there, when the chieftain
harshly defeated the Danes.

Tjodolv Arnorsson, *Magnusflokkr*, verse 23

CHAPTER 3

RELIGION, MYTH AND CULT

IN THE VIKING AGE, FAITH AND RELIGIOUS ACTS were referred to as '*forn siðr*'; ancient custom or 'religious custom'. There were no fixed beliefs, doctrines or dogmas in the Norse religion, such as you would find within Christianity or Islam, rather it comprised a multitude of performances and practical exercises. These customs concerned everybody in the community – everyone was born into the religious sphere.

There were many different supernatural powers for humans to relate to: gods and goddesses, jotuns (trolls or giants), dises, norns and valkyries, dwarfs, elves and goblins, to mention a few. The Norse gods and other powers required that people give worship and sacrifices, and recognise them as an unchanging, fixed part of everything, in order to avoid disaster. The Vikings were very superstitious and used amulets, magic formulas and sacrifices to remain on good terms with the supernatural powers. Everyone believed that the world was full of magical beings that one had to be friends with in order for things to go well. Together with the gods, the supernatural beings made sure that there was just enough wind, rain, frost and sunshine. If the relationship with the powers became unbalanced, there would be too much or too little of one vital ingredient, and that could become disastrous. Even the state of war or peace could be contributed to these powers. Warriors sacrificed to the gods and the powers for victory in warfare, while farmers sacrificed to fertility and weather gods to provide the right conditions for his crops.

It was the religious acts, that is, the rites and cultic acts, which enabled people to get in touch with the powers. A good relationship was a prerequisite for the wealth and prosperity of the individual, the farm, the family or the country. Each divinity and every power had their special qualities, and the motives for turning to them were equally diverse. A pregnant woman and her kin would call on the help of the dises, which are female powers connected to birth and to the protection of the family, while a crew on a Viking ship might ask the sea god Njord or Odin for protection.

There were several ways for the men and women of the Viking Age to communicate with the powers. The most common method for such communication is what the sources refer to as *seiðr*. We have no modern equivalent of the word, but sorcery or magic could be used. Along with, and included in the performance of *seiðr*, we have other forms of communication like *gandr*, which is the ability to cast spells, *galdr*, meaning repetitive songs or chants, and *útiseta* – 'sitting out' – involving a time of introspection in nature to receive a vision or to perform divination. Those who practised this might be called *shaman*, a modern word used about someone functioning as an intermediary between the ordinary human world and the spirit world. The shaman was able to alter consciousness for the purpose of gaining information, to seek council with the spirits of nature or the ancestors, to work their magic on behalf of the people, and to attend to the spiritual wellbeing of the community generally. Both men (*seiðmen*) and women (*seiðkona*) in ancient Norse society were able to practise shamanism or seiðr, but it seems to have been more common for women. There is something unmanly about the art of seiðr. A seiðman could be accused of being *ergi* and *arg*, which are two Old Norse terms of insult, denoting effeminacy or other unmanly behaviour and often used to refer to a man who engages in homosexual activities as the receiving part. This is something the Vikings thought particularly unmanly and shameful. It was, however, not seen as unmanly in the same sense if you were the male part in the relationship. The god Odin learned the art of seiðr from the goddess Freya. This shows us that Odin was a god that transcended all bounderies, even the strictest norms of society.

A woman who practised the art was known as a *seiðkona* or *völva,* which means 'wand carrier' or 'carrier of a magic staff'. Not everybody could become a successful shaman. Some people seem to have had better prerequisites to communicate with the powers than others. They were highly respected, and feared, members of the society. They were paid to perform different rituals, to heal the sick, help with childbirth, or to offer insight into what the gods and the powers thought about things. If you suspected that the spirits of dead people or other powers that did not belong to the farm collective had entered the boundaries of the farm, you could call a völva to drive them back out. In the *Saga of Eric the Red* we meet Torbjørg Lítilvölva ('the little völva'). She was a völva in Greenland and travelled around with an entourage of youngsters and children, who were her helpers. Around the year 1000 Greenland was undergoing a time of famine. The harvests were bad, there were no fish in the sea and some hunters had not returned. In order that people might know what the future would hold, the völva was summoned. Before her arrival the whole household was thoroughly cleaned and prepared. The high seat, which was otherwise reserved for the master and his wife, was furnished with down pillows for her to sit on. She appeared dressed in a foot-length blue or black cloak decked with gems to the hem. In her hand she wielded a wand, the symbolic distaff (*seiðstafr*), adorned with brass and decorated with gems on the knob. Around her neck she wore a necklace of glass beads, and on her head she wore a headpiece of black lamb trimmed with white catskin. Around her waist she wore a belt of amadou from which hung a large pouch, where she kept the tools used during the seiðr. On her feet she wore shoes of calfskin and the shoelaces had brass knobs in the ends, and on her hands she wore gloves of catskin, which were white and fluffy inside. As she entered the hall, the household greeted

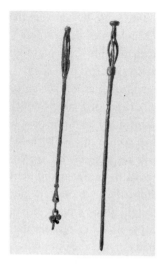

Two magic staffs, possibly belonging to a völva? The shorter one is from the Gävle area of Sweden and the longer from a grave at Fuldby, near Ringsted in Denmark. Photo: Arnold Mikkelsen, National Museum of Denmark, CC-BY-SA.

her, and then she was led to the high seat, where she was provided with dishes prepared especially for her. She had a porridge made of goat milk and a dish made of hearts from all the kinds of animals at the homestead. She ate the dishes with a brass spoon and a knife whose point was broken off.

The next day she would perform the rituals. In order to perform the seiðr, first she positioned herself on a special elevated platform and a group of young girls sat around her and sang songs intended to summon the powers that she wished to communicate with. The session was a success because the völva was permitted to see far into the future, and she foresaw the end of the famine.

The worship of the gods

There were two ways of worshipping the gods and the other supernatural powers. The first and most obvious was the central public cult, which included sacrifices. This generally took place at the chieftain's farms, at the thing assembly or at sacred places. The kings, earls or chieftains or maybe a designated cult leader called a *gode* led these ceremonies. In the sources a *gode* cared for the cult of specific gods in a designated place or cult building called a *hof.* The gode also had other social functions, such as lawman, a leader in war and trade, etc.

The second type of worship was the more personal type of cult activity that took place at the individual farms, led by the farm's

Head of Odin, found in Oslo, Norway. Photo: Ove Holst, National Museum of Oslo. CC-BY-SA.

representatives. The women were protagonists in the sacred acts that guarded the traditions of the farm and family, while the farmer led the ritual actions that marked the life of the individual family member. Then they served as a *gode* (male cult leader) and a *gydje* (female cult leader) performing the rites in the *blot;* the sacrifice or feast.

Some people and families seem to have had a closer relationship with individual powers. Some were worshippers of Frey or Freya, while others preferred Thor or Odin. Followers of the Odin cult, the Thor cult or the Frey cult had these deities as their *'fulltrudi'* - dearest friend, and attempted to achieve a

Two amulets representing Norse gods. Small statue of Frey, found in Rällinge in Sweden, and an ornamented Thor's hammer from Skåne, Sweden. Photo: Christer Åhlin, The Swedish History Museum. CC-BY- SA.

favourable relationship with them. The relationship between the different cults could be openly hostile and they could fight each other.

In the *Saga of Håkon the Good* we read that it was custom that the farmers came to the *hof* when sacrifices were held. Everybody had to bring with them all the food and drink they needed, including beer, and animals including goats, sheep and horses were slaughtered. With the blood of the animals they would colour the altar with the figurines of their deities, the walls in the cult building, both inside and outside, and all the people present. The slaughtered animals were then cooked and served to the guests. A drink would be carried around the fireplace, and the chieftain would bless the drink and all the sacrificial food. First they drank to Odin – for victory and power to the king.

The main cult events took place four times a year:
The winter sacrifice, held on October 14. It was
dedicated to the fertility god Frey and marked the
beginning of winter.

The midwinter sacrifice on January 12. It was
dedicated to peace, a good winter and a good
harvest in the coming year.

The summer sacrifice was held on April 14 and
marked the beginning of summer. It was devoted
to Odin and was held for victory in war and good
fortune on voyages.

The midsummer sacrifice was held around June
20, and was a festival of light, dedicated to the sun
and intended to keep evil spirits away.

Then they drank to Njord and Frey, for a good harvest and peace
(*Blóta til árs ok friðar*), which is a formula to promote health,
peace and good times for people and animals.

Human sacrifice

Today we know for certain that the Vikings from time to time
would sacrifice humans as well as animals, but we also know that
it probably was not a widespread custom. Human sacrifices and
ritual killings were carried out at funerals of important people
and major cult events, especially in crisis situations and times
of social stress. When animal sacrifice did not seem to work, a
human was the foremost offering one could give to the gods.
According to the *Ynglinga Saga*, the ultimate sacrifice the Vikings
could give to their gods was the king himself. But according
to other sources it was normally people of lower status such as

Scene probably depicting a human sacrifice to Odin. From the Stora Hammars picture stone in Gotland. Photo: Kim Hjardar

In the sources, *hug* and *ham* are two Viking terms for **the concept of soul**. The *hug* is most closely related to our modern idea of soul, but also incorporates notions of personhood, wish, desire and thought. Both gods and humans had the capacity, it was believed, to let the *hug* leave the body and transform themselves with an earthly disguise. Meanwhile your regular earthly body would rest or sit by idly. The *hug* then would take on a new *ham*, meaning skin. This ham could be in the guise of a strong bear, a noble eagle or an aggressive wolf, for instance. Some people were thought to have the ability to travel for long distances in animal guise and cause harm and do deeds. If you were *hugless* or *hamless*, you had been subjected to sickness caused by an ill-willed attack from others.

woman, slaves and children and probably also free men who were sacrificed. In Balleteare on the Isle of Man, beside the skeleton of a man who had been buried with a rich array of weapons and other equipment, there was a woman who had received a blow to the skull. In other cases, it appears that there are women who have been granted human victims – as in Dråby, Denmark, where a woman's grave also included the headless skeleton of a man. At Trelleborg in Denmark, archaeologists have found a cult place with what appears to be remains from human and animal sacrifice. In two pits there were child skulls, as well as skulls and bones from adult people and a lot of pig, cow and sheep remains. In Tissø on west Zealand archaeologists have found a farm with a cult place with remains of human bones, including a child's jawbone. There are also several other such finds among the Vikings. In war, human sacrifice also seem to be a custom. Byzantine sources describe how a Rus (eastern Viking) army buried their war dead by full moonlight, accompanied by mass executions of captured enemies.

The origin of the cosmos

The Vikings did not see time as cyclical, but as a straight line from creation to a future end. Norse mythology describes three ages: first the age before the creation of the world, then the age in which humans lived and when gods and giants kept the cosmos in balance, and lastly the age after Ragnarok, where the world will rise up after a cataclysm and turn green and fertile again.

According to the Norse myth of creation, cold and heat were the only things existing in the first age of the cosmos. To the north lay the icy realm of *Niflheim* and to the south lay *Muspelheim*, where a sea of fire filled the void. Between them there was only the gaping abyss of *Ginnungagap*, a realm of perfect silence and darkness.

The creeping frost from Niflheim and billowing flames from Muspelheim finally met in Ginnungagap. The fire melted the ice, and the drops formed themselves into Ymir, the first of the giants. Ymir was a hermaphrodite and could reproduce by himself. From Ymir, the giants were born. As the frost continued to melt, a cow, Audhumbla, emerged from it. She nourished Ymir with her milk, and she, in turn, was nourished by salt-licks in the ice. Her licks slowly uncovered Buri, the first of the gods. Buri had a son named Bor with a female giant, who again married Bestla, the daughter of the giant Bolthorn. The half-god, half-giant children of Bor and Bestla were Odin and his two brothers, Vili and Ve.

Odin and his brothers slew Ymir and used the body as a lid to cover Ginnungagap. From the corpse they constructed the world. They fashioned the oceans from his blood, the soil from his skin and muscles, vegetation from his hair, clouds from his brains, and the sky from his skull. Then they captured sparks from Muspelheim and formed the sun, the moon and the stars and gave warmth and light to their world. The gods eventually formed the first man and woman, Ask and Embla, from driftwood and built a fence around their dwelling-place, Midgard, to protect them from the giants.

As one can see there are similarities between this story and the biblical scene of the Garden of Eden and Adam and Eve. While the two stories must be connected, there is no notion of sin, shame or restriction put on the humans in Midgard. Another similarity is the notion of a cataclysmic end to the world, by deluge and war. But whereas the Christians believe they lived in the time *after* the great deluge, the Vikings believed they lived in the age *before* the great cataclysm. Their world would eventually perish in Ragnarok to make room for the third and last age. The end of time, or Ragnarok, which actually means 'end of the gods' was a central part of human understanding of reality – all things must die. But it must have been comforting to know that Ragnarok did not mean the end of life, but that a new era came after. The Edda poem *Voluspå* (The sorceress' prophesy) tells of a green and fertile earth that will rise from the sea, with roaring waterfalls and an abundance of fish and wildlife. Other sources

Audhumbla licking Búri out of rime, as four rivers of milk pour from her udders. From the 18th-century Icelandic manuscript SÁM 66 (Stofnun Árna Magnússonar á Íslandi) *now at the Árni Magnússon Institute for Icelandic Studies, Iceland.* CC-BY-SA

say that unsown fields would grow crops and no one would have to struggle for food – unlike the harsh reality people were so well acquainted with. Even the sun would be made anew. It is a bit like the Christian notion of Heaven.

This wood carving is from the Urnes stave church, near Kaupanger in western Norway. It is dated to the 11th century and might be depicting a scene from Ragnarok. CC-BY-SA

But before the world can rise again, the humans and gods have to endure the end of time, where brother fights against brother, and the gods fight the giants. Ragnarok begins with three years of war among people and gods. Then comes the Fimbul winter, an ice age where almost all living things die. There are also various horrendous natural disasters. The sea floods the land. Fenrir the Wolf breaks his chain; Naglfar, the death ship made of dead men's nails, breaks its anchor chain; Loki escapes from his prison and leads an army of giants against the gods. The dead Viking warriors dwelling in Valhalla have been training for this. They are drawn into action, and the great battle begins. Odin meets Fenrir the Wolf, Thor fights against the Midgard serpent, Heimdall battles Loki, and Frey fights against the fire giant Surt. But all is in vain; the world perishes in an apocalypse of death and disaster.

But from the ashes of this world a new world is born. Two humans, Liv and Livtrase, who survived the cataclysm, will be the source of a new line of human beings who will live in a world without war, deceit and devastating feuds, also something that the people of the Viking Age had to endure. Of the surviving gods, one of them, perhaps Heimdall, will become the new ruling god.

The Norse gods

The Norse gods did not care if they were liked by humans or not, but they expected humans to worship them and recognise their position in the cosmos. Humans had to come to terms with the gods if they wanted to avoid disaster. In this way, the Norse gods had many features in common with the Greek and Roman gods, who similarly required nothing beyond reverence from people.

The Norse religion did not have an evangelical purpose meaning that the religious message should be spread to other worshippers. Moreover, the Norse religion accepted that one could have several gods, including the Christian God and Jesus Christ. If a god appeared particularly powerful or if there was personal benefit to be obtained, a person could adopt a new god. The same principle also applied to human leaders, who lost their followers if they did not show themselves to be strong.

The theatre and symbolism of war were central to the Vikings' cosmology. The established order in the world of the gods was the result of a war. So it was important for people in the human world to worship powerful gods. The Norse gods and goddesses belong to two families of gods, the Aesir and the Vanir, who live together and form a cosmic whole. The sources of this arrangement can first and foremost be found in the Icelandic poet Snorri Sturluson's presentation of the *Ynglinga Saga* and in the poem *Skaldskaparmål*. These sources refer to a prehistoric war between the gods that ended in a peace settlement. Hostages were exchanged and thus the gods of the other party were incorporated. Three of the Vanir: Frey, Freya and Njord, who are fertility gods connected to sexuality, crops and times of peace, went to live with the more militarised Aesir in Asgard. Here the gods lived on their individual farms, mirroring the organisation of the world of the humans.

Odin is conceived as the first among the Norse gods and lives in Valhalla, a huge farm in the middle of Asgard. He is an old deity and is the same god as Voden, Wotan or Wodin, the old German divinity of war-fervour. Odin was a god with many faces

A list of the Norse gods

Aegir – a sea god associated with the ocean. He is also known for hosting elaborate parties for the gods. Married to Ran and lives under the waves. Aegir is a son of the giant Fornjótr (Ymir), and brother of Logi ('fire') and Kári ('wind').

Balder – god of light and purity, son of Odin and the goddess Frigg. Known as gentle and wise. Balder had the greatest ship ever built, named Hringhorni, and there is no place more beautiful than his hall, Breidablik.

Bragi – Norse god of poetry and eloquence. Son of Odin and husband of Idun.

Earth – daughter of Night and Annar.

Eir – goddess of healing.

Fjorgyn – lover of Odin and mother of Thor. Also referred to as Earth.

Forseti – god of justice. Son of Balder and Nanna.

Freya – main goddess of the Vanir (fertility gods). Daughter of Njord and sister of Frey. She is a goddess associated with love, sex, beauty, fertility, gold, *seiðr*, war and death. Freya rides a chariot pulled by two cats, and keeps the boar Hildisvíni by her side.

Frey – important god of the Vanir. Son of Njord and brother of Freya.

Frigg – main goddess. Wife of Odin and mother of Balder. Frigg is described as a goddess associated with foreknowledge and wisdom.

Gefion – fertility goddess. Associated with the plough. Tricked the king of Sweden out of a tract of his land.

Heimdall – watchman of the Norse gods and owner of the horn Gjall. Son of nine mothers. Often identified with Rig, the creator of three races of men. Will be the ruling god after Ragnarok.

Hel – ruler of Helheim, the realm of the dead.

Idun – guardian of the golden apples of youth and wife of Bragi.

Kvasir – the wisest god. Created from the spittle of the gods.

Loki – the sly trickster of the Norse gods. Son of two giants. Also known as the Sly One, the Trickster, the Shape Changer and the Sky Traveller. He is responsible for the death of Balder. Bound until Ragnarok.

Mimir – wise Aesir god. Sent to the Vanir to seal the truce between the two groups of the Norse gods. Killed by the Vanir, his head is kept alive by Odin.

Njord – a Vanir god associated with wind and sea. Husband of Skadi and father of Freya and Frey.

Odin – king of the Norse gods, and god of poetry, battle and death. Also known as the 'all-father', the 'terrible one', 'one-eyed' and 'father of battle'.

Ran – wife of Aegir. Drags drowning men down with her net.

Sif – wife of Thor. Her golden hair was cut off by Loki.

Skadi – goddess of winter and hunting.

Thor – god of the sky, thunder and fertility. Associated with law and order in Asgard. Son of Odin and Earth and husband of Sif. Also known as the 'thunder god' and 'charioteer'.

Tyr – a god associated with law and heroic glory in Norse mythology. He sacrificed his hand in the binding of the wolf Fenrir.

Ull – god of archery and skiing. Used to be the main god.

Vidar – son of Odin and the giantess Grid. Will avenge Odin's death after Ragnarok.

Amulet, probably of the goddess Freja, from Tissø in Denmark. Photo: Arnold Mikkelsen, National Museum of Denmark. CC-BY-SA

and abilities. He was the god of war, but also the god of ecstasy. You could be said to be possessed by Odin if you were drunk, enraged, insane, madly in love or in the heat of battle. The berserkers were associated with Odin, because they appeared to be possessed by him when in battle, taking no heed of pain, cold or heat. Odin also had a particular association with mankind's knowledge of both runes and poetry, a wisdom he sacrificed his eye to gain. One of Odin's attributes was his spear, Gungnir. For the Vikings, the spear was a symbol of enlightenment and of power justly applied, and therefore the symbol of a ruler. The spear also represented age and death. In Old Norse texts, Odin is depicted as one-eyed and long-bearded, frequently wielding his spear, and wearing a cloak and a broad hat. He consults the disembodied, herb-embalmed head of the wise being Mimir for advice. His animal companions often accompany him. Odin had in his entourage several animals with warlike connections: the wolves Freke and Gere, whose names signify bloodthirstiness, and the ravens Hugin and Munin, whose names mean 'Thought' and 'Memory'. In the skaldic poems, the ravens are referred to as 'the eagles of the battlefield,' because they gorge on corpses. Odin also has an eight-legged horse, Sleipner, who knows the road to the kingdom of the dead and carries the dead warriors there.

Odin had as many as two hundred different names, of which several are connected to war. Among others he was called Valfader

('Foster father to all who fall'), Seiersfader ('Father of victory') and Bolverk ('Perpetrator of violence'). The Vikings believed that many warriors who fell in battle were selected to go live with Odin; they were called *einherjar*. During the foretold events of Ragnarok, Odin is to lead the einherjar into battle before being consumed by the monstrous wolf Fenrir.

The second most important Norse god was Thor. He was a Germanic god of strength and the god of thunder and lightning, as the Greek Zeus and the Roman Jupiter had been in ancient times. Thor provides rain and is the watchman of the cosmos. Thor creates life, whereas Odin takes it away. Because he constantly fought with the giants and had extraordinary strength and courage, he was also seen as a war god. Thor had many more human characteristics than Odin (who was seen as fickle and capricious), and was preferred by many as a more concrete and personal divinity. Thor's hallmark, the hammer, was popular in the late Viking period as an amulet, worn by warriors and others – perhaps also as a contrast to the Christian cross?

Odin's warriors – berserkers and wolfskins

The berserkers and 'wolfskins' were a special group of warriors associated with the god Odin. Their description in the sources is on the periphery between fantasy and reality, and it is difficult for us to imagine that such people ever truly existed. Berserkers and wolfskins are distinguished by their ecstatic battle fury and incontrollable destructive power. According to the sources they could muster inhuman strength, and when they attacked they howled like mad dogs or wolves. It was said that neither iron nor fire could injure them and that they did not know pain. After a battle they were as weak as infants, totally spent both physically and mentally. They developed as a brotherhood of professional itinerant warriors who would take up service with different chiefs. What distinguished them was that they saw bears and wolves as sacred animals, and clad themselves in their skins.

Mythological realms of the Norse gods

Alfheim – the land of the light elves in Asgard.

Asgard – land of the Aesir.

Bilskirnir – Thor's hall in Asgard.

Bifrost – the flaming rainbow bridge between Asgard and Midgard.

Breidablik – Balder's hall in Asgard.

Brime – hall of the giants in Utgard.

Eljudnir – Hel's hall in Niflheim.

Fensalir – Frigg's hall in Asgard.

Folkvang – site of Freya's hall in Asgard.

Gimli – the most beautiful hall in Asgard, where the survivors of Ragnarok will meet.

Helheim – the realm of the dead in Niflheim, ruled over by the monster Hel.

Himinbjorg – Heimdall's hall in Asgard.

Idavoll – the central plain of Asgard. Contains the halls of Gladsheim, featuring thirteen high seats where the male Aesir hold council, and Vingolf, where the goddesses gathered.

Jotunheim – land of the giants.

Midgard – the realm of mankind.

Mimir's Well – well of wisdom under the root of Yggdrasill in Asgard. Guarded by the head of Mimir.

Muspelheim – southern land of fire guarded by the giant Surt.

Niflheim – land of freezing mist and darkness and home of Hel.

Sessrumnir – Freya's hall in Asgard.

Sindri – red gold roofed hall which will appear after Ragnarok.

Svartalfheim – realm of the dark elves.

Thrudheim – Thor's realm in Asgard and site of his hall Bilskirnir.

Thrymheim – stronghold of the giant Thiazi, father of Skadi.

Utgard – realm in Jotunheim ruled by Utgard-Loki.

Valaskjalf – Odin's hall in Asgard.

Valhalla – hall presided over by Odin where the einherjar await Ragnarok.

Vanaheim – land of the Vanir in Asgard.

Vigrid – plain in Asgard where the final battle will occur.

Vingolf – hall of the goddesses in Asgard.

Ydalir – Ull's hall in Asgard.

Yggdrasill – the world tree.

The berserkers often comprised an elite troop in addition to the main guard or army. In sea battles they were usually stationed at the prow, to take the leading point of an attack. In the Battle of Hafrsfjord they appeared as shock troops for Harald Fairhair, fighting in groups of twelve.

In 1784 a priest called Ödmann started a theory that going berserk was the result of eating fly agaric mushrooms (*Amanita muscaria*), but considering how poisonous this is, it is quite unthinkable that it would be eaten. The most probable explanation for going berserk comes from psychiatry. The theory is that groups of warriors, through ritual processes carried

Berserker depicted on a chess piece from the early 12th century. Found on Isle of Lewis, Scotland. CC-BY-SA

out before a battle (such as biting the edges of their shields), would go into a self-induced hypnotic trance where they acted on direction; they kill enemies. The Old Norse social order and religion were able to accommodate this type of behaviour, and it is understandable that the phenomenon disappeared after the introduction of Christianity. A Christian society considered such rituals and actions as demonic and thought that they must have resulted from supernatural influences.

Realms of death

The Vikings belived that life would continue after death, and that the quality of the afterlife would reflect your status and conduct while living. Snorri Sturluson says in *Ynglinga Saga*, that 'the dead should be burned on a pyre together with all their possessions, and that everybody would arrive in the afterlife with such wealth as he had with him on his pyre and that he would also enjoy the use of what he himself had hidden in the ground.'

In Asgard there were several 'warrior paradises'. Dead warriors could dwell with Odin in Valhalla, or they could serve in Freya's hall, Folkvang, where half the warriors collected by the valkyries ended up. Freya has the right to choose first who will come to her, and those who are chosen are usually more honourable and less bloodthirsty than those who are taken to Valhalla. A third warrior's paradise in Asgard was the hall Gimli. Here only the most just and honourable warriors would gather when they died. It is described as the most beautiful place on earth, with roof made of red gold. It is also the main assembly hall in Asgard. At Ran, the sea goddess' place, those who were lost at sea would reside. Ran has fishing nets that she uses to catch the dead sailors. She is married to Aegir. Aegir's hall is a holy place where grand feasts are held, and it was considered a good thing to be with Ran and Aegir. When drowned people appeared as revenants, it was seen as a good omen, because this was a sign that they had been well received by Ran. Another realm of the dead was Brime, the feasting hall of the giants in Utgard. Here there was always enough to drink. There is also a realm in the land of the dwarfs. Their hall, Sindri, is made of red gold, and is the home of the educated and good. In Niflheim there is a realm called Hel or Helheimr, which is ruled by the mistress Hel, sister of Fenrir the wolf and the Midgard serpent. Odin once ventured into Hel and found a hall prepared to receive the god Balder. The benches were covered with chainmail, and the pillows were adorned with gold. There was much mead to drink, poured from barrels covered by shields. It was almost the perfect warrior paradise. Those who died of old age or sickness could reside here. But not all realms were to be desired. In Niflheim, there is also a huge and terrible hall, with its doors turned northwards towards the icy winds. The roof is made of braided snakes, and their heads is turned inwards and they spew venom at the inhabitants. In the rivers of venom that run through the hall oath breakers and outlawed murderers wade for eternity. But the worst of all is to be cast into the well of Kvergjelme. Here the dragon-like serpent Nidhogg resides and nourishes itself on the bodies of those condemned to be ghosts for eternity. What you had to do to deserve this fate is not quite certain, but betrayal and cowardice could lead to a terrible afterlife.

But the realms of death could also be close to where people lived on earth. Almost every farm of a certain size had one or more burial mounds where important family members were buried and lived out their afterlife. In Iceland there also seem to have existed a notion that the dead lived inside a nearby mountain. Torolv Mosterskjegg and his family believed they would continue their existence inside Helgafjell (the Holy Mountain), and thus be close to the farm and the rest of their kin. To continue to serve the family in this way was considered a good death. The Vikings had a notion that the dead in the mound or mountain were still a part of the farm community, and that they kept track of what happened outside the mound

Burial mound from Borre in Vestfold, Norway. Only very mighty men and woman were given graves like this one. Photo: Kim Hjardar.

and could protect the farm and the people living there. The ship in the famous Oseberg burial mound in Norway was anchored to a huge boulder, maybe to keep the ship and its passengers in the mound, so that the community could benefit from their presence. Those who reside in the mounds are not seen as spirits or ghosts, but as real living dead, almost like vampires or zombies. Sometimes they come out of they mound to assert revenge for a crime or an offence, or to give advice or gifts to the living. Although they are mostly seen as an asset, they could be quite troublesome at times and wreck havoc on the living,

Graves laid out as ships from Lindholm Høje in Denmark. They would originally have been covered by soil. Photo: Kim Hjardar

by killing and maiming both humans and cattle. We hear of actions taken by the living to control the unruly dead, their mounds would be opened up and the bodies reburied, moved, cremated or beheaded. If one could not contain the unruly dead or ghosts, one had to move away from the farm. The *Laxdaela Saga*, written down in the 13th century, tells of the troublesome Rapp, who wrecked havoc after his death. Rapp was a violent ghost, and he killed most of his servants and tenants. The entire Rappstad farm was laid desolate through Rapp's ravages. Before he died, Rapp had told Vigdis, his wife, that he had to be buried standing right up and down under the doorstep of the firehouse on the farm, so he could keep up with what was happening. Now Vigdis took the initiative to dig up the dead Rapp, and the body was then put in a stone mound in a remote location, far from Rappstad. Nevertheless, the ravages continued, and it was not until the body of Rapp was dug up again and this time burned on pyre and the ashes scattered on the sea, that the ravages finally ended.

How were the Vikings buried?

Mortuary rites in Scandinavia during the Viking Age are puzzling. Only about half of all the people who died seem to have been accorded a formal grave at all. Funerary rites seem to only been given to people of a certain status, and the rest was cremated and their ashes scattered and not given a formal grave. Snorri Sturluson says in *Ynglinga Saga* that everybody is cremated but that only notable men would get a monument like a mound or memorial stone erected in their honour. The very poor and the slaves maybe did not get any funerary treatment at all. The Arab writer Ibn Fadlan says in the 10th century that dead slaves of the Vikings were simply abandoned, and children, with some exceptions, are also missing from the archaeological burial record.

But for those who did get buried, two different types of burial practice dominated. Cremation, that is, burning the dead to ashes before burial, and inhumation, which means burying the dead without burning the body first. Throughout the Viking Age, cremation was the most common practice in Scandinavia, while inhumations were much rarer. In most cremations the person was burned while fully clothed and given grave goods such as ships or wagons, weapons, jewellery, and implements of different kinds of production and food preparation. Also horses and riding equipment, different animals, furniture, food and drink and many other objects were burned with the dead. The ashes would then be either strewn over the ground or at sea, or covered with an earthen or stone mound or laid to rest in a chamber grave. They could also be placed inside an urn or vessel of some kind.

Several written sources suggest that the soul of the dead was more easily released through fire and that the flames speeded up the transition to the realms of the dead. Cremation has also been interpreted as a way for dead warriors to come to Valhalla. Some scholars are looking at cremation as a kind of food offering to the gods. Additionally, it was a way to protect the living against diseases and odours associated with the dead body.

Inhumation graves are rarer, but they have provided posterity with the most spectacular finds from the Viking Age, and without them our knowledge of the Vikings would be limited. The bodies were generally laid in rectangular graves, either directly into the ground or in coffins of various kinds, such as a boat, wagon, chest or chamber. Inhumation burials often include an even greater range of grave goods than cremations. In the richest tombs, in addition to the dead and their personal equipment, we find ships, horses and other animals, and in some cases even remnants of people who have joined the dead in the grave. We know from both written and archaeological sources that people were ritually killed to be buried alongside the dead. Such cases are found in both cremation and inhumation burials.

A number of graves incorporate unusual practices that are difficult to interpret. Both in Sweden and Norway there are examples where spears or axes seem to have been thrown into the grave while it was open, perhaps in a form of ritual surrounding the funeral. In some graves, the body appears to have been quartered before the burial. The funerary rites of the Viking era were diverse indeed, and our understanding is often enshrined in mystery and lack of knowledge and sources.

CHAPTER 4

PLUNDER, EXPLORATIONS AND SETTLEMENTS

Early raids

WHEN SCORES OF SEABORNE RAIDERS APPEARED on the English coast in the late 700s, it seemed as though they had sailed out from hell itself. But it was no coincidence that the Vikings came to England. The onslaught had been brewing for a long time. For the Vikings, war was everywhere. Their society was highly militarised, honour was everything and losing one's reputation was worse than death. Offending another man's honour could only be resolved through combat or blood revenge. Combat was part of the fabric of Viking society and it was raw and brutal, like all warfare at that time.

The wars brought by the Vikings led to major upheavals in Europe – among other things, they played a part in the unification of England under one king, prepared the way for the development of the northern European nation states, gathered the fragmented northern lands into independent nations, and laid the foundations for the kingdom of Russia in the east.

In most history books, the Viking Age began on 8 June 793. On that summer's day, Vikings attacked the monastery on the island of Lindisfarne off the north-east coast of England, stole its treasures and killed its monks. This incident is well documented in the *Anglo-Saxon Chronicle* and in letters sent by clerics. But it was not the first time warriors from Scandinavia had haunted those shores. In the summer of the year 789, three ships from Hordaland in Norway landed on the Isle of Portland on the south coast of England. Here the crew began to extort tolls from passing ships and claim support from the fishermen and the farmers living on Portland and the nearby mainland. The king's bailiff went to the coast with the intent to bring the strangers to King Beorhtric's bailiff in Winchester so that tolls could be collected from the trading goods they surely had with them. The meeting ended with a fatal confrontation when the Norwegians killed the bailiff and his men. This was the first time in recorded history that seafaring Scandinavians had resorted to an act of violence, and these dreadful events became widely known in the Christian world. Three years later came the first defensive action against the Vikings when King Offa of Mercia organised a coastal defence in Kent, most likely against Viking piracy.

The first raiding bands consisted of anything from a single ship's crew of 30–40 men up to groups of 400. They used unorthodox and unpredictable strategies, especially by combining land and sea operations, which were difficult for more organised forces to contend with. While under sail, the Viking ships would normally stay out of sight from the land. When the time came to launch the attack, they would lower the mast and row quickly towards the coast or up the rivers. Without their sails, the low and narrow Viking ships could be almost invisible until they were right on the coast. Their shallow keels enabled them to land almost anywhere. The most important element for the Vikings' success was their basic strategy – outflank the enemy by approaching from the sea, and attack rapidly and forcefully, with yelling, screaming and clashing of weapons to paralyse the enemy with fear. Prior to the attack, the Vikings reconnoitred the area and identified the target. The attack had to happen quickly, so as not to scare away the booty of slaves to sell and high-ranking people to ransom, and to thwart attempts to organise a defence. The attack would preferably take place early in the morning, before the population had properly started their daily routine. The whole operation would only take a few hours. It was not unusual for people to be killed in the course of these raids, but outright executions of people who were unsuitable either for the slave trade or for ransom were not as frequent as the Christian sources would suggest.

When they reckoned they were done, they set fire to the place and withdrew. The Vikings believed that if you burnt down the buildings you plundered, you could feel confident that spirits would not follow you home to wreak revenge. Fire was considered the best defence against sorcery and dark forces.

Why did they attack?

Since the Bronze Age there had been frequent contact between the Nordic countries, the British Isles and the European continent. Excavations both in the Nordic countries and elsewhere testify to such interaction and indicate that it was mainly of a peaceful nature. Towards the end of the 8th century, however, the relationship changed and became characterised by violent attacks. There is no simple answer to explain this change, since it is linked to social changes both within the Nordic countries and outside.

In western Europe, both Emperor Charlemagne in the Frankish empire and King Offa of Mercia, the greatest kingdom in England at the time, had brought prosperity and peace. Ports and cities were open for trading. Wars only occasionally interrupted the general peace. Nobody seemed to have feared invaders from the sea, and coastal defences had either been demolished or were non-existent in large areas of France and England.

Meanwhile, in the early Viking Age, Scandinavia was divided into a range of smaller kingdoms, lands, counties and legal districts ruled by chieftains and petty kings. From the late 700s power became concentrated in fewer hands. European culture and politics gave examples and inspiration for petty kings and big men to gather more power into their own hands. A growing population required more stable and durable political institutions. Control of lucrative trading links and sites gave the chieftains and kings greater power and more wealth and status. At the same time, the age-old cult of Odin was in decline, and many disillusioned young men needed to find other ways of expressing themselves, just when the elite, who had access to resources in the form of ships and armed men, felt the need to operate in wider arenas. This may have been an important factor for the waves of attack against Europe at the beginning of the 9th century.

Some have thought that population pressure lay behind the Viking expansion. For Norway's part, this can be explained in marginal areas, for example in the western part of the country, where the cultivation of new lands was minimal or impossible. But it was only in the later part of the Viking Age that there was a large relocation from Denmark to occupied areas in England, the Danelaw, and to the areas of Normandy in France. The North Sea Islands, Iceland and Greenland were colonised mainly by people from western Norway, but not until the second half of the 9th century.

The Nordic communities in the Viking era were militarised societies with a strong honorary code. Undertaking successful raids against adjacent regions normally won honour. In the early Viking Age it was considered particularly honourable for Vikings to kill enemies in war. Killing people outside one's own region gave more glory, while 'home' murder was considered a crime and called for punishment and revenge. A stronger central power in Scandinavia meant controls on behaviour were increasing. The system of penalties and punishments set up in parliamentary assembly at the thing and the concentration of power made it difficult for young men to earn themselves honour, renown and consequent social advancement. As that gradually became more difficult, the hunt for honour may have pushed the Viking voyagers further abroad to find fame and fortune.

According to old Germanic tradition, the usual arrangement was for a kingdom to be divided and shared among all the sons, but during the Viking Age it became more and more important to keep the kingdom together. The challenges were therefore many and bloody, and many men of high rank were forced into exile with their followers, often re-appearing as leaders of Viking bands in

France and England. When the central powers in these lands failed to repel the attacks and protect their holy places and inhabitants, they were seen as easy targets. The amount of valuables, slaves and honour brought back from these raids made a great impression on the Scandinavians and spurred on more attacks.

Not being Christians, Vikings did not respect the values of the Christian world and did not see churches and monasteries as holy places. People in the north had completely different values from people in Christian Europe. This is why until the Norse countries became Christian, it was ideologically, religiously and ethically unproblematic for the Vikings to attack Christian holy places. And it was defenceless churches, monasteries and trading ports who became victims of the earliest Viking attacks. The attacks were seen as a punishment from God. Archbishop Wulfstan of York wrote this passage to explain the Viking raids:

> The Englishmen have for a long time suffered complete defeat and been despondent because of God's anger; for the pirates are so strong with his consent that just one of them often drives ten to flight in war … all this because of our sins … what else can be the cause except God's anger clear and visible over his people?

From the *The Sermon of the Wolf to the English*, 1014

The shock felt when such assaults began was enormous in Europe, mainly because it was directed against the religious institutions. However, it had nothing to do with Viking persecution of Christians or any particular hatred toward Christians. The fact that the Vikings in many cases left the monks and priests alive, and in some cases paid compensation to monasteries when murders occurred, indicate that Christianity itself was not the target, but that the Vikings had material goals. The reason why monasteries were seen as particularly attractive targets was that they were readily accessible and contained wealth. They were usually not fortified, and those that were did not mount much of a defence. In addition to being a potential source of slaves, the monasteries were rich in loot. Candlesticks, crucifixes, silver vessels, book fittings, gold clasps and jewelled reliquary casks must have given Vikings gold fever. Many archaeological finds in Scandinavia provide evidence that the Vikings who started plundering monasteries found great profit in their enterprises, and we can assume that the booty financed many a chieftain's ambitions. The treasure hunt led to a race between different groups to find the monasteries first, with the result that many establishments were plundered frequently and repeatedly. The response in many cases was that religious communities either disappeared or moved to safer locations.

During the course of the eleventh century the pattern of attacks changed. From frequent quick raids of plunder, they went on to become fewer, but more powerful acts of conquest. This was a result of the kings strengthening their monopoly on power in Scandinavia. This led to the loss of many of the traditional sources for recruitment of warriors. Military service for the kings and their allies gradually became the only way one could make a career as a warrior. In turn, the kings became more and more dependent on conscription of free farmers. One such example was Harald Hardrada's unsuccessful invasion attempt of England in 1066. His forces consisted primarily of his own own professional troops, called up through Harald's nobles, but he also had a large proportion of warriors enlisted through warship conscription. Kings with political goals now led the attacks on Europe.

Head of a memorial stone supposedly depicting the attack on the monastery of Lindisfarne.

CHAPTER 5

EXPANSION IN THE NORTH AND WEST

When Vikings from Norway set sail and crossed the sea at the end of the 8th century, they arrived at the Orkneys and Shetlands. In the course of only a few years, these islands went from being a den for pirates and refugees from the power struggles in Norway to becoming one of the greatest Viking centres of power and the seat of the Earls of Orkney.

Orkney and Shetland were strategically situated for sailing both to Norway and to the British Isles. With a favourable wind it took little more than twenty-four hours to sail from Hordaland on the west coast of Norway to Shetland. The fjords and inlets around Shetland provided good, well- protected harbours for the Viking ships and soon became important bases for voyages of both plunder and trade: north to Norway, north and west to the Faeroe Islands, Iceland and Greenland, and south and east to England and Ireland. The islands became a central hub in the network of Viking trade routes between Norway, England, Ireland, Iceland and Greenland.

The soil on the islands was rich, fertile and easy to cultivate. In the 10th century, there were 300–400 farms and around 2,000 Norse settlers on the Orkneys, and about 200 farms and 1,200 settlers on Shetland. Groups of sea pirates and traders also visited, lodging in camps along the coast.

The Hebrides are often also considered to have been part of the Earl of Orkney's domain. Their Old Norse name was Suðerøyene ('the Southern Isles'), in comparison with the Orkneys and Shetland, which were and still are referred to as the Northern Isles. These areas was initially dominated by a people called the Picts, but the Vikings did not seem have a high regard for them. In an anonymous work, *Historia Norwegiae* from around 1190, we find a rather derogatory description of the Picts. They were referred to as 'pygmies' and considered cowards. Many of the Pictish chiefs on the islands fled over to the Scottish mainland, but around 839 almost all of the Pictish nobility in Scotland was killed in a big battle against the Vikings. This greatly weakened the Pictish kingdoms, which were soon destroyed.

Independent centres of early Norse power also rose on the Hebrides. In 853 a man called Kjetil Flatnose was lord of an area which in addition to the Hebrides and the Isle of Man included parts of Skye, Mull and Islay. All these had been part of the old Pictish coastal kingdom of Dalriada, until Kjetil drove out the last remains of Pictish power and established himself as ruler. Two groups formed the basis of his power. He had support among the Vikings who had settled on the Hebrides and, perhaps most importantly, from a group known as the Gall-Gaedhil ('Foreign Gaels'). These were people who in many ways lived in two worlds, one Norse and one Celtic. They had Celtic-Nordic ancestry, and even though they lived among the Vikings, they had their own chieftains and their own laws and political ambitions. The Gall-Gaedhil emerged in many places, but mainly in Ireland and in the Norse colonies around the Irish sea. Wherever the Vikings came, people of mixed ancestry began to appear.

The Orkney earls

The rise of the Orkney earls began when a powerful Norwegian warlord, Ragnvald Earl of Møre (*c*. 866–*c*. 870) passed control

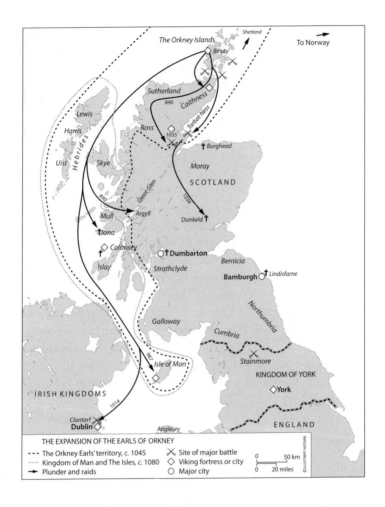

THE EXPANSION OF THE EARLS OF ORKNEY
- - - The Orkney Earls' territory, c. 1045   ✕ Site of major battle
· · · · Kingdom of Man and The Isles, c. 1080   ◇ Viking fortress or city
→ Plunder and raids   ○ Major city

0   50 km
0   20 miles

of the Orkney Islands to his brother, Sigurd the Great, who through widespread warfare extended the realm into mainland Scotland. He transformed the islands from being a peripheral part of Norway's archipelago to become a centre of power in the northern part of the British isles. The earldom rose during a turbulent time in Norwegian history. One of Ragnvald Earl of Møre's main opponents in Norway was the emerging power of

Harald Fairhair, the first unifier of Norway. Harald's sons had attacked Ragnvald's power base in Orkney and one of them had been killed. This prompted an all-out invasion of the island by Harald, who demanded compensation of 60 gold marks from the Orkney inhabitants as payment in recompense for his son's killing. As there was no way the islanders could pay such a huge sum, they themselves now risked being killed. Einar, nephew of Sigurd the Great, offered to pay the whole sum himself in exchange for being allowed to continue as earl, while recognising Harald as his supreme king. Harald agreed to this and so confirmed Einar's status as lord over the isles. Einar used his new authority to set about a comprehensive military organisation of his territory. This enabled him to keep control of large parts of his uncle Sigurd's Scottish mainland kingdom. Einar ruled with a firm hand right up to his death, some time between 910 and 935, and he was succeeded by his sons, Arnkjell and Erlend. Under Einar's rule, the Orkney Isles became an important link in trade routes from York and Dublin, over the Norwegian Sea to Norway and over the Atlantic to Iceland and Greenland. The Orkney earls also had dynastic and diplomatic links with kinsfolk in Normandy and with other Norse colonies in Ireland, the Isle of Man and the Hebrides.

In the middle of the 930s Harald Fairhair's youngest son, Håkon Adelsteinsfostre (meaning: foster son of King Athelstan), drove his brother Eric Bloodaxe from power in Norway. Eric and his family ended up on the Orkney Islands, where he gained power from Einar's sons. They in turn became Eric's closest supporters, and were present when he took over the kingdom of York in 948. Both were killed alongside Eric in 954. It is not clear how the power structures in the region evolved after Eric Bloodaxe left the Orkney Isles. There are signs to suggest that the centre of power moved away from the Orkneys and that another powerful island kingdom with headquarters on the Hebrides developed around 970.

The descendants of the Earls of Møre continued to govern the island realm until 1137, followed by a new line of earls until

1455, when the islands were given as dowry for the marriage of Christian I of Denmark and Norway's daughter to King James III of Scotland. After having been part of both the Norwegian and the Danish kingdoms, they were incorporated into the Kingdom of Scotland in 1470.

The kingdom of the Isle of Man

The centre of power soon shifted from the Hebrides to the Isle of Man. The kingdom of Man and the Isles, as the new entity was soon called, was divided into five semi-independent areas which sent their representatives to a central parliament, the Thingvollr (Tynwald) on The Isle of Man. This kingdom survived more or less intact as a political entity until 1095. We first hear about permanent Viking control over the Isle of Man in about 918, when the by then Dublin-based Vikings invaded Anglesey and probably also the Isle of Man. From then on, this big island with its central location was a strategically important piece in the Vikings' struggle for control of the Irish Sea. The best known of all the kings of Man and the Isles is Gudrød Crovan. He is the first king to be described in the *Chronicle of the Kings of Man and the Isles*. Gudrød was the son of Harald Svarte ('Harald Black') who was from Islay (or possibly Iceland or Ireland, depending on interpretation). According to some reports, Gudrød took part in the Battle of Stamford Bridge in 1066, fighting on Harald Hardrada's side, and sought refuge on the Isle of Man after the defeat. Gudrød won the island for himself in the Battle of Skyhill in 1079, and made it the ruling seat for his family right up to 1277. After Gudrød's death the Norwegian king, Magnus Barelegs, who thought that the Norwegian crown had a historic claim to the region, challenged the kingdom's independence. Magnus followed up the claim with military force in 1098. However, when he was killed in 1103 the region fell under the influence first of the Irish and later of the English kings. The Scandinavians' physical dominance of the region was over, but Nordic traditions and language survived for hundreds of years. The Isle of Man inherited the Vikings' legal system and still has its Tynwald today.

The rise of the Dublin kings

The most important story of Viking activity in this region, however, is that of Ireland. Sometime in the 790s, the Viking fleets operating round the north coast of Scotland and the Hebrides came to Ireland. It is uncertain where exactly these Vikings came from. Both Norwegian and Danish Vikings were

Head of a Viking warrior from the Oseberg ship burial. Museum of Cultural History, Oslo.

navigating the Irish Sea at that time, the Norwegians from the north via the Hebrides and the Danes from the south via the English Channel. The Irish annals for 795 relate that there were accounts of attacks on the island of Rathlin off northen Ireland and Inishbofin and Inishmurray off western Ireland. In the years following the first attacks, numerous monasteries were ravaged repeatedly. The Norwegian Vikings voyaged ever further south, and Kerry in south-west Ireland was the target of an attack in 813. However, Viking activity is thought then to have diminished gradually as there quickly began to be fewer

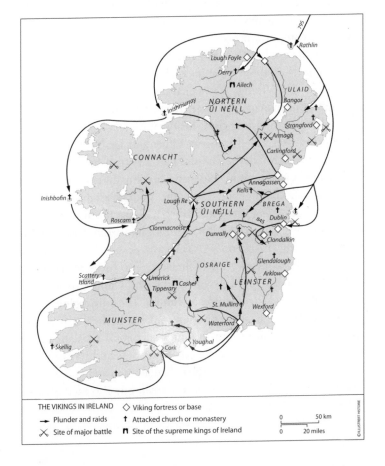

THE VIKINGS IN IRELAND · ◇ Viking fortress or base

→ Plunder and raids · † Attacked church or monastery

✕ Site of major battle · ⋔ Site of the supreme kings of Ireland

0   50 km

0   20 miles

easily accessible targets. Instead they had to travel inland to find booty, which made them vulnerable to counter-attack, and there are reports of a series of defeats by the Irish kings. Another reason for the let-up was that the Vikings were busy elsewhere, as they began to colonise the Hebrides. When the Vikings arrived, Ireland was divided into over 150 independent kingdoms, which in turn belonged to six supreme kings. Strong local loyalties prevented the Irish from coming together in a single kingdom and co-ordinating their defence against the Vikings, but this also prevented the Vikings from gaining control over large territories in Ireland. The Vikings were soon both willing and unwilling participants in the never-ending Irish power game.

The most important event related to the Vikings' activities in Ireland is the establishment of the trading centre of Dublin. In 836 two fleets of about 60 ships each arrived at the rivers Liffey and Boyne. The Vikings who sailed up the Boyne met with stiff resistance, but managed to force their way into Lough Erne and plunder the surrounding countryside of Meath.

The other fleet sailed into the Liffey and landed near a little village called Ath-Cliath. The site had a perfect harbour, could be defended easily without expensive investment and was a short sea journey from England. Here, the Vikings established what the sources call a *longphort*, a fortified harbour for the longships. The place was named Dyflin, or Dublin (from Irish 'Dubh Linn,' meaning 'black pool'). This was to be first in a series of fortified harbours set up in Ireland. The fortified harbours opened the rivers to fleets of Viking ships and exposed the interior of Ireland to widespread plunder. The only region where permanent Viking bases were not set up was in the north, where the Irish kings managed to mount a successful resistance. The Vikings estabished a series of petty kingdoms and power bases, like Waterford, Wexford, Limerick, Annagassen and many more. From here, they not only fought the Irish, but also each other.

Another important event in the chronicles of the Vikings in Ireland is the arrival of a powerful Danish-Norwegian alliance that came to Ireland in 852 to take over from the divided Viking factions. The leader of this alliance, Olav the White has been connected to the Norwegian kings from Borre in Vestfold. He arrived with two members of the Danish royal family, Ivar (Imar) the Boneless and Åskjell (Oscytll). In 853, Olav the White declared himself supreme king of Dublin and of all the Vikings in Ireland – Norwegian and Danish. At the same time, Ivar took control of the Vikings in the west of Ireland by annexing the base in Limerick. The status of Olav and Ivar as men of royal lineage helped them not only to gain control of the Norwegian and most of the Danish Vikings, but also to receive support from many of the Irish minor kings. The arrival of Olav and Ivar marked a new phase for Ireland and the whole region around the Irish Sea. Olav's ambition was to dominate the Viking colonies in the region, by political means as much

Vikings arrive on a ship. Image from the Gotland picture stone at Stenkyrka. Photo: Kim Hjardar

Cast of a male figure from Irish bucket handle found in the Oseberg ship burial. Evidence of Viking riders in Ireland at the beginning of the 9th century. Photo: Erik Irgens Johnsen, Museum of Cultural History, Oslo

as military. He was particularly known for forming alliances by marriage. At the end of the 850s he tried to gain control of the Hebrides by marrying Aud the Deep-minded, daughter of the greatest Hebridean chieftain, Kjetil Flatnose. The alliance proved to be short-lived, when Kjetil and the Gall-Gaedhil soon afterwards attacked several places in Ireland. Olav gradually expanded his area of power to include the whole of Kjetil's earldom. By 871 Olav controlled most of the areas round the Irish Sea and he brought masses of booty and numerous slaves to the markets in Dublin. Then he disappears from the sources, but was followed as king by Ivar who is thought to be the founder of a royal dynasty in Ireland known as Uí Imar, which held on to power till 1035.

Through invasion and terror followed up by the building of alliances, Olav and Ivar had succeeded in taking control of a large kingdom stretching from Northumbria in England to Dublin and the other Viking towns in Ireland and including parts of Scotland, the Hebrides and the islands in the Irish Sea as far as Wales.

The disappearance of Olav and Ivar from the political scene in Ireland left a power vacuum which led to a decade of internal strife among the Vikings there. Taking advantage of this political chaos, the Irish came together under the leadership of Cerball of Leinster and expelled the Vikings from Dublin in 902/3.

The social effect of this first Viking period on Ireland has been difficult to measure. There is no doubt that the Vikings were responsible for the ruinous decline of monasteries and church life at this time. On the other hand, there is no indication that the attacks led to a setback for Christianity and its hold on the population. Despite extensive persecution and plundering by the Vikings and Gall-Gaedhil, the church institutions were strong enough to withstand the pressure. There are also indications that the extent of the plunder and the consequences for individual religious centres have been somewhat exaggerated by the chroniclers. We see the same tendency in all the other parts of Europe visited by Vikings.

Return to the Emerald Isle

The Vikings in Ireland went from being totally expelled by the Irish to reconquer their domains with force in 917. But throughout the 10th century internal squabbles between mainly the Dublin and the Limerick Vikings led Irish kings to assert their power over the foreigners. This second phase culminated with the ascent of Brian Boru from Munster to the title of supreme king in Ireland, and a spectacular showdown with the Vikings in 1014. Later chroniclers describe the Battle of Clontarf in 1014 as the culmination of two hundred years of fighting for power between the Vikings and the Irish.

Coin minted by Sigtrygg Silkbeard. The inscription reads SIHTRC REX DIFL, 'Sithric king of Dublin'. Creative Commons.

Sigtrygg Silkbeard (king 989–1036) was the first of Dublin's kings to mint coins (997). He was the result of an alliance between the Viking king of Dublin, Olav Kvåran and the kings of Leinster. His mother, Gormflaith, was a Leinster princess. She was later also given away in marriage to Máel Sechnaill, king of Uí Néill, to strengthen the new alliance between Leinster and Uí Néill. With support from his stepfather Máel Sechnaill, Sigtrygg worked to re-establish Dublin's hegemony over the Vikings in Ireland and to halt the advance of Brian Boru. But in 997 the power struggle between Máel Sechnaill and Brian Boru took an unexpected turn. They made an agreement to share Ireland between them, and at the same time created an alliance to drive the Vikings out of Ireland once and for all. Brian was considered to be the more potent of the allies, and the people in Leinster were not happy that their king had submitted to king Brian Boru of Munster. So he was deposed in 998 and replaced by Gormflaith's brother, Máelmorda mac Murchada, who led a rebellion against Brian's authority.

Sigtrygg Silkbeard had also ended up under Brian's control but by 999 he had had enough of this. With support from Máelmorda, he also started a rebellion against Brian. But Brian and Máel Sechnaill's combined army succeeded in pushing Sigtrygg back to Dublin. Brian then besieged the town for 20 days before storming it. The inhabitants were afflicted with famine and lack of water, and the streets were full of wounded Vikings and Leinster Irishmen. Sigtrygg submitted to Brian and was reinstalled as king in Dublin and obliged to enter into a peace treaty and alliance with Brian. To seal the new deal, he had to marry one of Brian's daughters. For his part, Brian married Sigtrygg's mother, Gormflaith, who was divorced from Máel Sechnaill. In this way both the Dublin Vikings and Leinster came under Brian's influence.

With the help of Sigtrygg and the Vikings, Brian Boru finally succeeded in establishing himself as Irish Supreme King in 1002.

The bloody field of Clontarf

Slightly before 1012, Brian had divorced Gormflaith, who was probably no longer important for alliance politics. The chronicles record that from then on, she used all her time to urge her brother, Máelmorda, and Sigtrygg to revenge themselves against Brian. In 1012 rumours were circulating of a new rebellion led by Máelmorda and Sigtrygg. Brian again laid siege to Dublin in 1013, but Brian's forces ran out of supplies and the siege was lifted around Christmas time. The rebellion came to a surprising end when Máelmorda recognised Brian as his superior king. The Leinster king had to bow to political reality, and Brian Boru was still the strong man of Ireland.

Sigtrygg's rebellion continued, however, and the alliance which he was building grew fast. Sigtrygg's son, Olav, got support from the Norse colonies in Galloway. On the Isle of Man, the powerful Earl Brodir acknowledged Sigtrygg as his superior king and promised him military support. Sigurd the

Great, Earl of Orkney, supported Sigtrygg, because Brian also threatened his regional dominance. As a counter move Brian Boru mobilised all his minor kings and his allies, including Vikings from Limerick and the Hebrides. His predecessor, Máel Sechnaill, brought 1,500 men from Meath. Brian's assembled army amounted to 7,500 men. Towards the end of April 1014 this huge army surrounded Dublin and closed all roads around the harbour town.

Inside Dublin, Sigtrygg had also gathered a formidable force. He himself had 2,000 well-equipped Dublin warriors. Sigurd came with 1,000 Vikings from the Orkney Isles and Brodir with 1,000 from the Isle of Man. Máelmorda rallied 3,000 poorly equipped men from Leinster.

On the night of 22 April the Vikings of Dublin landed their army on the shore at Clontarf on the north side of River Liffey. By this manoeuvre the Vikings managed to choose the site of battle, which is always strategically important, and they gained time to organise themselves.

The Viking alliance set up for battle with their backs to the shore but Sigtrygg himself had at the last moment opted out of taking part himself, and stayed in Dublin with 1,000 warriors. Nobody knows why he decided at the last minute to stay away from a battle he had been working towards for years. Perhaps he wanted to protect the population and the wealth in Dublin against a possible overwhelming attack by Brian? Perhaps he had secretly accepted payment from Brian to stay away, as some sources claim? Whatever the explanation, it was his son Olav who represented him on the battlefield.

Máelmorda drew up his lightly armed troops from Leinster on Olav's right. The men from Orkney gathered in the middle under Sigurd's raven banner. Sigurd was the real leader of the army in Sigtrygg's absence and the one who by dint of his seniority and experience must surely have laid out the main strategy. Brodir stood on the right flank with the men of Man.

Brian didn't take part in the battle either, but stayed behind in his tented camp with a small guard troop. His oldest son

Murchad mac Brian led the Munster alliance. Máel Sechnall also refused to take part in the battle and placed his men on a high point to the left of the field, where they would have a good view of events. So there were a good 6,000 men on each side on the plain at Clontarf.

The Viking alliance had the upper hand at first. Their experience in battle and their strong weapons forced Murchad's line to swing back, but it did not break. Only the Viking mercenaries on the Irish right flank held position and repelled the Dublin Vikings. On the Dublin Vikings' right flank, Brodir started a storming attack, but ended up in a personal duel with Ulf, Brian's brother-in-law, and was knocked unconscious. Murchad's Munster men were elite troops, and all their leaders had some sort of family tie with Brian. Half of them pressed hard on Brodir's leaderless troops and forced them back to their ships on the shore. Among the losses in this action was Murchad mac Brian himself.

Sigurd's and Máelmorda's men faced the rest of the Munster men and gradually began to gain advantage over them. But Sigurd's raven banner was like a magnet to the enemy, who constantly stormed the shield wall round the standard bearer and the earl. In the end they broke through, and Sigurd's standard bearer was cut down. A fallen banner signifies defeat, and the warriors in the ranks became uneasy. So Sigurd grasped the banner himself and raised it. The Irish cut him down and killed him a few minutes later.

When evening came, the Viking alliance was in a grave situation. Both flanks had broken, Sigurd had been killed and Brodir was injured. Ulf controlled the shore. Many threw themselves into the sea elsewhere and tried to swim out to the ships, often drowning as a result. Olav and a bigger group tried to fight their way out to retreat to safety in Dublin. Máel Sechnaill saw how things were heading and now threw himself into the fight. He blocked the bridge over the Liffey, and Olav Sigtryggsson and nearly all the surviving leaders of the Viking alliance were killed in the fighting which followed.

Brodir and a handful of warriors had sought shelter in a copse not far from the town. There they discovered Brian's relatively undefended camp and stormed the king's tent. The watch was outnumbered, and Brian was cut down by Brodir himself, according to the Irish sources. However, Brodir's forces were soon outnumbered and Brodir was taken prisoner. Ulf killed him in a gruesome manner, as revenge for his killing of Brian.

It is impossible to reckon the losses in this battle, but it is estimated that only a fifth of the Viking army survived the battle and the subsequent massacres. None of the Viking leaders survived apart from Sigtrygg who had stayed in Dublin. On the Irish side, somewhere between 1,600 and 4,000 were killed, in addition to both Murchad and Brian Boru himself.

The defeat at Clontarf did not immediately change the political situation between Irish and Vikings, nor Dublin's status as the regional power-centre. Sigtrygg was still alive, with several thousand men around him. Brian's death, however, led to the raise of Máel Sechnaill as supreme king and the collapse of Munster's hold on the Norse and Irish settlements around the Irish Sea. The Danish king Canute the Great was fighting his way to power in England and stood ready to fill the vacuum and several of the southern Viking colonies and their leaders, including Sigtrygg, recognised him as their superior.

Sigtrygg died in 1042, probably aged over 70. His impact on the area was formidable. In the 990s he introduced coin-minting in Dublin and towards the end he established a bishopric in the town. But on the broader scale, the end of his rule can seen to be an significant stage in the decline of Viking power in Ireland. Sigtrygg's departure marked the end of Dublin's position as the leading Norse centre in Ireland, though the town continued to be an important pawn in the continuing conflict between the kings in Munster and Leinster. Dublin would survive as an independent kingdom until 1171, but after Sigtrygg the kings were mostly Irish, or members of various Viking dynasties which were well integrated with the local royal families and had become more Gaelic than Norse.

CHAPTER 6

THE ONSLAUGHT IN ENGLAND

As WE SAW, THE FIRST RECORDED visit to England by Vikings was in the summer of 789, when a group of Norwegians landed on Portland and started demanding tax from the local population and passing ships. However, it is the attack on the Holy Island of Lindisfarne, the most sacred place in England, on 8 June 793 which is the most famous and which has been used to define the start of the Viking Age. The event was recorded in the *Anglo-Saxon Chronicle* for the year 793:

> Fearsome warnings came over Northumbria, terrifying the people. There were intense lightning flashes, and people saw terrifying dragons flying through the sky. These signs were followed by a great famine and later the same year on 8th June hordes of heathen men tragically laid waste God's church on Lindisfarne by plundering and killing.

The attack is also recorded on piece of a stone cross, which was probably raised in memory of the dead after the Viking attack in 793. The stone shows what appears to be a group of attacking Vikings. On the other side there is a motif of the Day of Judgement. Many people interpreted the attack as a sign that Doomsday was imminent. The attack was also interpreted as an assault on Christendom itself. Gruesome tales of the Viking ravages on Lindisfarne spread throughout Europe. The pirates had not only plundered the monastery for valuables, but had also killed monks, smashed everything they found, including holy relics, and abducted several of the monks to a life of slavery. The person who was most enthusiastic in explaining the attack as a divine punishment for the nation's moral shortcomings was the monk Alcuin from York. He was one of the most influential spiritual thinkers of the day and adviser to the Frankish King Charlemagne. Alcuin was hoping that news of the attack could lead to a strengthening of the weak political position of the church in Northern England. It is an early example of the use of propaganda and spin, but it seemed to work.

The third recorded attack on England itself was against the monastery at Jarrow, just south of Lindisfarne. At Jarrow, however, the Vikings met tougher resistance than anticipated, and their leaders were killed. Bad weather caused several of their ships to founder off Tynemouth, and the local population killed all the survivors they found. After this there was a sudden pause in Viking attacks on England. If the annals are to be believed, the Vikings stayed away for the next thirty years.

The most important reason for the scarcity of attacks is that in Scotland there was still a strong Pictish kingdom which could keep southbound Vikings at a distance. The Vikings concentrated their efforts instead on the Scottish coast, the Hebrides, Ireland and the Isle of Man.

When the Vikings finally returned in force to England in 835, they came from France, from Ireland and directly from Scandinavia. Their reasons varied; they now often turned their attacks on England when they were under pressure in France or had been paid to stay away. The Vikings in Ireland raided England for both economic and political reasons. There were many lucrative targets to be plundered, and they often tried to gain control of regional trade. England was the closest target if you travelled via the Orkney and Shetland Isles and did not fancy your chances in either Ireland or Scotland. The political situation in England was unstable since it consisted of five more or less independent kingdoms. Until 830, the king of Mercia was considered supreme king in England but the ambitious kings of Wessex gradually took over this position. The Vikings often took advantage of the many conflicts between the Anglo-Saxon kingdoms and between the Anglo-Saxons, the Britons and the Celtic population in northern and western England.

The early years of the Vikings' interaction with England are mostly hidden in the mists of history, but for every attack on England where a record has been preserved in the written sources, there must have been numerous attacks that went unrecorded. The few that we know of are mainly the ones suffered by the kingdom of Wessex, because that is where the written sources mostly come from. Even these have many years without any mention of attacks. But we know from French sources that the Vikings were active in the English Channel and must have had easy access to England also in those periods.

Vikings attacked London for the first time in 842. The town on the Thames was at that time not a capital city, but an Anglo-Saxon trading centre, controlled by the king of Wessex and rich in goods. From London, one could also control both access to the interior of southern England via the Thames, and export routes to overseas. Following the Viking attack, the Roman town walls were restored and extended, in the hope of being able to stop the Vikings.

From around 850 the Vikings began to over-winter in England, first on the Isle of Thanet, a peninsula at the eastern tip of Kent, and then in many other places along the coast. Another tradition that came to England at that time was the paying of Danegeld. In 865 the Vikings were offered payment to go away from a district for the first time. A small Viking army which had settled on the Isle of Thanet negotiated with the local population to accept silver and valuables in exchange for abstaining from plundering.

The Great Viking Army arrives

The most important event in this first phase of the Viking onslaught on England was the arrival of a Viking army of

The Great Heathen Army arrives in England, as illustrated in the Life, Passion and Miracles of St. Edmund, *c. 1130. Pierpont Morgan Library. MS M.736, CC BY-SA.*

between 2,000 and 5,000 warriors. In the sources it is called the *Great Heathen Army*, and it nearly managed to conquer the whole of England. It arrived in East Anglia in the autumn of 865 and was not there merely for plunder, but to conquer the land and settle there. According to the *Anglo-Saxon Chronicle* this army was led by Ivar (Imar), Halvdan and Gorm (Guthrum) who probably belonged to various branches of the Danish royal family. Using brutal co-ordinated attacks supported by well-grounded intelligence information and rapid advances and retreats, the army came within a hair's breadth of crushing all organised resistance in England.

After receiving the East Anglians' submission and tribute at Thetford in Norfolk, the army built fortified winter quarters in Thetford. In autumn 866 the Great Heathen Army followed Ermine Street north to York, where they took the town on 1 November without having met serious resistance. In 866 York was the seat of one of the two archbishops in England and the richest trading centre north of London. It was strategically situated in the fertile agricultural land of today's Yorkshire and was accessible by sea through the rivers Humber and Ouse. The town offered the Viking army both a choice of escape routes if need arose, and access to a rich surrounding countryside with great opportunities for plunder. Under its new name of Jorvik, York would gradually become the most important Viking town in North England. Halvdan installed a puppet king, Egbert in Northumbria. He was to govern 'until the time when Ivar and Halvdan would return', and a garrison of Vikings was installed to watch over him, before the army went on to Nottingham where they besieged and stormed the town. King Burgred of Mercia and his brother-in-law, King Ethelred of Wessex led their armies to Nottingham and tried to urge the Vikings to come out of the fortress and face them in open battle. The Vikings declined the offer and the outcome was a peace treaty whereby Mercia paid the Vikings to go away and granted them safe passage through Mercian territory and back to York.

By the autumn of 869 the Vikings returned to East Anglia, where after an 'orgy of plunder and violence' according to the chroniclers, they came in late autumn to Thetford and prepared to over-winter there. King Edmund of East Anglia gathered his troops for a final showdown with the Viking army, but at Hoxne in November 869 the Vikings annihilated the last remains of Edmund's forces. The king himself was taken prisoner and killed. East Anglia became divided into several petty Viking kingdoms.

Halvdan led the army towards Wessex in summer 870 and captured the town of Reading, near the Wessex border, and set up a fortified base there as a starting point for systematic plundering of the surrounding area. But almost immediately after their arrival in Reading the Vikings were attacked by a local unit of conscripted troops from Berkshire under the leadership of the king's ealdorman (earl) Ethelwulf, at Englefield. Bands of Vikings out plundering were forced back to the camp, which was then surrounded. Four days later, King Ethelred and his brother Alfred arrived with the main army. A bigger engagement followed on 4 January 871, when Ethelred launched an unsuccessful attack on the Viking camp. Ethelwulf, who had put the Vikings to flight only a few days earlier, was killed in the fighting.

A series of bloody battles between the Vikings and Ethelred followed, starting at Ashdown only four days later. The battle did not go well for the Vikings. One of their leaders, Bagsecg, fell, and Halvdan had to retreat with great losses. Despite their defeat at Ashdown, the Vikings still held the initiative in the war, and already on 22 January the two armies clashed again, at Basing. This time the Vikings won, so decisively that for the next two months they could plunder Wessex without fearing Alfred and Ethelred. A new battle took place between Ethelred and Halvdan in March at a place referred to in the sources as Merantun, 9 km south-west of Marlborough, Wiltshire. In this battle Ethelred was killed and the English suffered a painful defeat. The *Anglo-Saxon Chronicle* summarises the year 871 thus: 'This year nine big battles were fought against the plundering army in the kingdom south of the Thames, in addition to innumerable skirmishes which Alfred, the king's brother, a single ealdorman and the king's thegn fought.' The new king, Alfred, asked the Viking army for a truce, and surprisingly Halvdan accepted the request. But Wessex was the only kingdom which had offered the Viking army significant resistance. This had probably surprised the Vikings, who were accustomed to local defence rapidly falling apart. The campaign in Wessex had already cost the lives of at least one Viking king and nine earls, in addition to hundreds, perhaps as many as a thousand, warriors killed or injured. It is perhaps not so surprising that Halvdan accepted the offer of a truce. His own army was on the verge of collapse, and a pause in the warfare was a welcome chance to lick his wounds.

The Vikings drew back to Mercia and settled in London for the winter of 871–72, and in the spring they withdrew to Northumbria. The next year Mercia also fell to the Vikings when the capital town of Tamworth was sacked and King Burgred fled. The new puppet king, Ceowulf, swore solemnly that he placed himself and the kingdom at the disposal of the Vikings. The chronicle describes him as a 'stupid servant'. The Vikings now controlled three Anglo-Saxon kingdoms: East Anglia, Northumbria and the eastern part of Mercia, and they had brought mighty Wessex to its knees. At this moment, at the height of its power the Great Heathen Army divided itself. Halvdan went north to take control of the rest of Northumbria, while Gorm continued the war against Wessex.

Throughout occupied England, little villages with Scandinavian settlers gradually grew up at the same time. Many of the settlers were warriors and their wives, who left the Great Heathen Army and settled down as farmers. Others were newcomers from Scandinavia and the islands in the Western seas, seeking a fresh start in life.

Gorm launched his attack on Wessex in spring 876. The Great Heathen Army advanced more than 250 km to Wareham in Dorset without meeting any resistance at all, and there was no serious resistance when they plundered the western part of the kingdom. Alfred managed in the end to get together a counter-offensive strong enough for him to negotiate a peace treaty with Gorm. The negotiations started at Wareham, where the Vikings

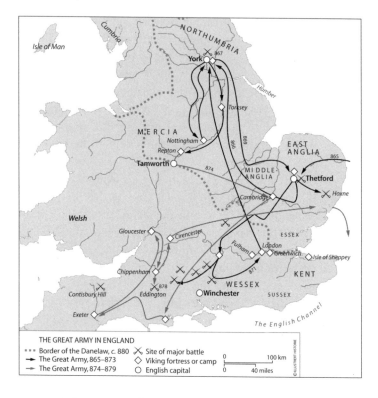

THE GREAT ARMY IN ENGLAND
- - - Border of the Danelaw, c. 880
→ The Great Army, 865–873
→ The Great Army, 874–879
✕ Site of major battle
◇ Viking fortress or camp
○ English capital

0   100 km
0   40 miles

accepted the terms and 'swore oaths on the holy ring.' The terms were that they must leave Wessex. But halfway through the negotiations, the Viking army broke out of Wareham and set course for Devon. With Alfred in pursuit, they captured Exeter and barricaded themselves in there. Gorm's unexpected march was in response to news that a big Viking fleet had reached the coast of Devon and was heading east. Gorm's plan was to revitalise his offensive by uniting with this fleet. However, a storm dispersed the fleet and several ships sank. Without these expected reinforcements, the Viking army was now isolated in Exeter. Alfred offered them a new agreement and this time the Vikings also had to hand over a number of prominent people as hostages.

Gorm withdrew to Gloucester to rearm. At the same time about 1,000 warriors had over- wintered in south Wales, and now planned a co-ordinated invasion of Wessex in the winter of 877–78. Gorm attacked Dorset and Somerset, while a fleet of 23 ships was to land in Cornwall and join up with Gorm's forces somewhere inland. But in the Battle of Contisbury Hill 800 warriors from this force were killed and 'their sacred raven banner captured', as the chronicle said. Gorm in the meantime had succeeded in subjugating large parts of Wessex. King Alfred's army was on the point of falling apart, and he had no alternative but to make a strategic withdrawal to the marsh districts around Athelney in Somerset. Gorm's warriors, confident that they had achieved a comprehensive victory, did not pursue Alfred but instead started a ruthless campaign of plundering.

The English strike back

From his involuntary exile in the marshes, Alfred organised a resistance campaign and rebuilt his army by recruiting men from Somerset and Wiltshire and the neighbouring parts of Hampshire and giving them intensive training. He eventually managed to bring about a decisive engagement between the Vikings and his fresh, well-motivated troops in open battle at Eddington in Wiltshire. The Vikings were put to flight and pursued back to their fortress at Chippenham where Alfred besieged them for two weeks, until Gorm had no other option but to accept a new peace offer. In addition to the usual oaths and hostages, Alfred extended the terms this time by requiring Gorm and his leading men to submit to baptism. Gorm was given the Christian name Athelstan and solemn oaths were sworn about the terms of the withdrawal. A final and formal peace treaty eventually came into force between Gorm and Alfred. Alfred got nominal control of London and all the country west of Watling Street, the old Roman main road. The boundary, which ran along the Thames, northwards up the river Lea to Luton, straight on to Bedford and then along the river Ouse to Watling Street, divided Anglo-Saxon England from the region which later came to be known as the Danelaw, the region which was governed by Danish law. Gorm had managed to create a Danish realm in England.

But the boundary was moveable and the peace fragile and the Vikings set up five fortified support bases in the main development areas wich gradually came to be known as 'The Five boroughs': Derby, Leicester, Lincoln, Nottingham and Stamford. York continued as the capital centre and was also the starting point for colonisation throughout Northumbria. Those members of the Great Heathen Army who did not want to settle down and earn a peaceful livelihood went instead to France or Ireland. Many historians have praised Alfred as a great strategist and England's liberator. In fact, the Vikings' grip on England was stronger after Alfred's death in 899 than it had ever been before. They had secure footholds in Northumbria, East Anglia and East Mercia, and they were constantly threatening Wessex and Kent. But even though the Scandinavians in the Danelaw had a shared culture and country of origin, they were not at all a united people. In the north there was a kingdom which more or less corresponded to the original Northumbria, with York as its capital. This was the best organised of the Viking realms in England. East Anglia consisted of at least two small 'mini-states' each with its own king: an older state with a seat in Thetford; and a younger one with a seat in Colchester. East Mercia, or Danish Mercia, consisted of at least nine independent chieftainships, each with its own fortress and army.

Alfred's descendants were key people in the old Anglo-Saxon kingdoms which were still independent. His son Edward the Elder inherited control of Wessex. Alfred's daughter, Aethelfled, was married to King Ethelred of West Mercia. Edward's son, Athelstan, followed him as King of Wessex. Over the next forty years, Wessex would take control over the whole of England south of the river Humber, and even the Viking kings in York eventually had to acknowledge that the king in Wessex ranked above them until they also were finally expelled in 954.

The Vikings return

The struggles against the Vikings in the middle of the 10th century led to England developing into a strong, military-based kingdom. After the Viking kings of York were driven out it would be almost 30 years before new groups of Vikings again tried their luck in England, but in 980 they came back. Internal power struggles in Denmark and Norway forced many chieftains and their warriors out of the countries, and now many of them the appeared in England. The first big wave of attacks was against the east and south coasts. The Vikings were mainly out for slaves and booty to carry away. But the situation changed dramatically around 990, when the Danish King Svein Forkbeard and the ruling elite in Denmark were forced into exile by the Swedish king Erik the Victorious, and started to lead plundering raids along the coasts of Kent and Essex. The rumours of the booty to be had in England, Wales and Cornwall also reached the ears of a petty Norwegian king's son, Olav Tryggvason, in exile in Russia. He led a powerful fleet which included Vikings based in Russia and the Baltic. The two warlords formed an alliance and divided England between them. Olav's greatest victory was the defeat of the English in the Battle of Maldon in the autumn of 991, the first major battle between the Anglo-Saxons and the Vikings for almost 60 years. After the defeat King Ethelred (the Unready) made a decision which would turn out to be disastrous for himself and for England. He offered Olav Tryggvason 10,000 pounds of silver to take his army away from England. This was the first in the series of payments of silver to the Vikings from King Ethelred. Even though the army was now being paid to refrain from plundering England, there was nowhere outside England where they could settle safely, so they stayed. The English hatched a new plan

Viking dragonhead from the Oseberg ship burial. Photo: Ove Holts, Museum of Cultural History, Oslo. (The original background is removed)

in the winter of 993–94. Instead of yet again paying the fleet to leave, they would now pay them to remain in England and protect the country from other potential enemies. The agreement between Olav and Ethelred that came about specified that peace would prevail between the Vikings and the English, and that the Vikings from now on would protect the country against invasion and foreign powers. It also set up a number of regulations about how Englishmen and Vikings should relate to each other, both in England and if they met or participated in joint operations beyond Ethelred's realm. Olav and his men were given fine gifts and 22,000 pounds of gold and silver. The agreement included an absolute requirement that Olav and the Vikings who were present at the great ceremony would submit to being baptised. Ethelred himself was godfather to Olav.

The agreement gave England some sorely needed breathing space. Olav ravaged around the Irish Sea in the years 994–95.

Little is known about what Svein and his Vikings were doing in the meantime, but the fact that they appear to have been calm and peaceful suggests that they too had benefited from the treaty. Svein was able to return to Denmark and reclaim the throne in 995. Olav Tryggvason also went home in 995, to become king of Norway. However, most of the combined Danish-Norwegian-Slav Viking army stayed on in England.

The Viking genocide

In the years that followed, the remaining Vikings had broken their agreements with Ethelred on almost every occasion since the peace treaty was signed, and conducted plunder and raids in the country. So on 13 November 1002 Ethelred struck against what he saw as a threat to his kingdom, in what later came to be known as the St. Brice's Day Massacre. He had been planning a countrywide genocide of all Scandinavians in the kingdom, including his mercenary army. Thousands of settlers, farmers of Scandinavian ancestry, women and children were killed by furious mobs of citizens all over England. There are reports that churches where people had taken refuge were set on fire and the victims burnt inside. Nobody knows how many people were killed, but among the dead were thousands of settlers and mercenary soldiers.

The Danish king Svein Forkbeard was among many who lost family members in the atrocity, and the demand for vengeance was soon so strong that Svein equipped a fleet and sailed to England in 1003 and ravaged the country. New plundering armies followed almost every year, but the beginning of the end for Ethelred's kingdom came in 1006, when the first of several enormous Danish plundering armies landing in England. A surviving rune stone erected in the memory of a man called Ulf (Wolf) provides a clue to who led some of this armies. The runes tell that Ulf was in England three times and gained wealth. First he came with Tostig in 1006, then with Torkjell the Tall in 1012 and finally with Canute the Great in 1015. We can form an idea of the size of the army that first came in 1006 from reports that all arms-bearing men in Wessex and Mercia were called up, but that the English avoided confronting the Vikings in a direct battle because they did not feel strong enough.

The conquest of England

Torkjell the Tall led several large fleets from Denmark. According to tradition Torkjell belonged to the Jomsviking order of mercenaries and brigands established by Svein Forkbeard's father in the 970s. So we can assume that Svein initiated and supported the plans. Among the young Viking chieftains who accompanied Torkjell on his big expedition in 1009 was the future king of Norway, Olav Haraldsson (Olav the Holy). Ethelred had to pay up again and Torkjell the Tall disbanded his army in 1012, after he had been paid 48,000 pounds in silver. He and Olav, accompanied by 45 ships and their crews, then went into mercenary service for Ethelred.

Svein Forkbeard personally led an invading army to England in 1013. Torkjell at Ethelred's side as a mercenary weakened Svein's position in England. Svein probably felt he had no choice but to go over to England himself. Svein established his headquartes in Gainsborough, and potentates and chieftains from the Five Boroughs, from Mercia, East Anglia and from Northumbria came and swore loyalty to Svein. Svein's son Knut (Canute) was married into one of Mercia's leading families, undoubtedly with the purpose of legitimising Svein's claim to England. The populace might accept him as their king more easily if they saw that he had support from one of the greatest families in the land. Svein then led the army to Lincoln, which became his new headquarters. The great towns of Northampton, Oxford and Winchester fell like dominoes, without a struggle. King Ethelred sat in London and Svein tried several assaults on

A spectacular English sword from the first half of the 11th century found in a Viking grave in Langeid, Norway. Photo: Vegard Vike, Museum of Cultural History, Oslo.

the city, but Ethelred and Torkjell's men fought hard. Among other things, London Bridge was set on fire to prevent the Vikings from crossing. Svein got nowhere and he returned to Gainsborough for the winter. During the winter Ethelred fled the country and Svein was formally declared king of England around New Year's Eve 1014. But only days later on 2 or 3 February Svein Forkbeard died unexpectedly of a heart attack and his newfound kingdom rapidly fell apart, as Ethelred, Torkjell and Olav returned and reconquered the land. Only a small part of Svein's army, led by his son Canute, were holding

London. According to the saga it was Olav the Holy who personally saved the day for Ethelred. The Englishmen and their Scandinavian mercenaries had tried without success to storm the fort protecting London Bridge. Olav's little fleet of ships, protected by roofs improvised by weaving bits of timber and branches together, went in under the bridge and tied the ships to the posts with ropes. Then the ships were rowed away and by force of raw muscle power the bridge crashed into the sea, weighed down by the swarms of Danish Vikings. With the route up the Thames now open to Olav and Torkjell's fleet, the Vikings in London had no choice but to surrender.

Ethelred became seriously ill during the year 1015, and his sons fought for power. Canute now decided to invade England again. He reckoned that large parts of the mercenary army would change sides, considering it more profitable to support a strong Scandinavian king than a weak English one. Only four months after making landfall in Wessex he had subdued both Wessex and Mercia, and on 1 January 1016 he entered Northumbria.

When King Ethelred died on 23 April 1016, the Wessex aristocracy chose Edmund (Ironside) as the new king of Wessex. Canute was recognised as king in Mercia, East Anglia and Northumbria. But Canute's ambition was to rule the whole of the kingdom of England, and he advanced south. The war between Canute and Edmund ended unexpectedly. In the autumn, the Vikings crossed the mouth of the Thames and plundered Essex and the neighbouring parts of Mercia. Edmund followed them with his army and caught up with them near Ashingdon in south-east Essex. There, it was agreed that the armies should at last meet for a decisive battle. The field of battle was on and around a small hill covered with ash trees. Canute drew up his army on the top of the hill, among the trees.

Edmund formed his army into a dense shield wall. This kilometre-long wall of men, with their spears out in front, then started moving slowly up towards the Vikings. From behind, the English archers shot volley after volley of arrows over the ash

Canute the Great and Queen Emma present a cross to the church in Winchester. From Liber Vitae c. 1031, British Library, Stowe MS 944, ff 6r-7r. *CC-BY-CA*

wood. Canute closed himself in behind his own shield wall and awaited the attack. The Vikings were accustomed to attacking with clamour, jeering shouts and resounding horns, but the English moved in step and in silence and didn't start their war cries until they were a spear's length away. The exhausted

Englishmen stormed into Canute's massive shield wall with their last bit of strength, aiming for his black and white raven banner.

At the same time, the Vikings launched their counter-attack on Edmund's banner. The lines weaved back and forth, without either of them breaking. But as soon as the fighting began in earnest, the whole of Edmund's flank withdrew from the battle. The English lost the battle and Edmund himself was wounded in the fighting but survived.

Edmund and Canute finally came face to face on Alney Island in the River Severn near Deerhurst. They met and exchanged hostages and words of friendship, and discussed dividing the kingdom between them. Canute would rule all the land north of the Thames, while Edmund would rule south of the Thames. London would function as a sort of no-man's-land and would be governed by dowager Queen Emma. When Edmund Ironside died in November 1016 while still a young man, Canute was officially declared king of all England. There are indications that Edmund may have been murdered, but Canute's name is not mentioned in connection with his death. With Canute established on the throne in England, the classic Viking Age was over. Adventurers still came wanting to serve in Canute's retinue, and from time to time there were local disturbances and risings, which had to be suppressed. But major plundering raids inland and coveted payments of silver were no longer possible.

Canute's network of alliances and his military leadership gave him unsurpassed control of Scandinavia and the British Isles. He was so dominant that neither Scandinavian royal pretenders, Orkney earls nor Irish kings could challenge him. He was the 'Emperor of the North'. However, the basis of his power was personal, and like many such personal kingdoms it held together only so long as the king lived. The Anglo-Danish kingdom established by Canute dissolved soon after his son, Harthacnut, died at the age of only 23 in 1042. With the death of Harthacnut, the Anglo-Danish kingdom in England died before it had been thoroughly established. A later attempt by Svein Estridsson, another grandson of Svein Forkbeard, to restore the Anglo-Danish realm also failed. The Norwegian king Magnus Barelegs' invasion of the kingdom of Man and the Isles, and Ireland, which cost him his life in 1103, was the last aftermath of the Viking kings' ambition to create a North Sea empire.

The reign of the Raiders of the Sea had come to an end.

SOURCES

PRIMARY SOURCES

Adam av Bremen (1994). *Beretningen om Hamburg stift, erkebiskopenes bedrifter og øyrikene i Norden*. Translated by B.T. Danielsen & A.K. Frihagen. Oslo: Aschehoug.

Chronicles of the Kings of Man and the Isles (1995). Translated by G. Broderick. Manx National Heritage.

Den legendariske Olavssaga (2000). Translated by K. Flokenes. Stavanger: Erling Skjalgssonselskapet.

Den Norsk-Islandske Skjaldedigtning. Vols A I-II, B I-II (1912–1915). Finnur Jónsson (ed.). Copenhagen and Kristiania: Gyldendalske Boghandel/ Nordisk Forlag.

Edda-dikt (1993). Translated by L. Holm-Hansen (2nd revised edition). Oslo: Cappelen.

Fadlan, I. (1981). *Risala*. I: J.B. Simonsen (ed.): Vikingene ved Volga. Højbjerg: Wormianum.

Fagerskinna: Norges kongers ættetavle (2007). (ed. Titlestad, T.) Translated by E. Eikill. Stavanger: Saga Bok.

Gulatingslovi (1952). Translated by K. Robberstad. Oslo: Det Norske Samlaget.

Hirdloven til Norges konge og hans håndgangne menn (2000). Translated by S. Imsen. Oslo: Riksarkivet.

Historia Norwegie (2003). Ekrem, I., Mortensen, L. B. (ed.); Fisher, P. (translator). Copenhagen: Museum Tusculanum Press.

Norrøn saga I–V (1989). Oslo: Aschehoug.

Orknøyingenes saga (1970). Translated by Anne Holtsmark. Oslo: Aschehoug

Porphyrogenitos, C. (950). *De administrando imperio*. Translated into English by Jenkins, R.J.H. (1949–62). Budapest.

Rimbert. (1926). *Ansgars levnad*. Translated by G. Rudberg. Stockholm.

Soga um jomsvikingane (1931). Translated by Albert Joleik. Oslo: Samlaget.

Sturlason, S. (1978). *Den yngre Edda* (*Gylfaginning*). Translated by E. Eggen. Oslo: Det Norske Samlaget.

Sturlason, S. (1970). *Heimskringla*. Translated by A. Holtsmark & D. A. Seip. Oslo: Gyldendal Norsk Forlag.

Tacitus, C. (1968). *Agricola og Germania*. Translated by T. Width. Oslo: Aschehoug.

The Anglo-Saxon Chronicles (2000). Translated by M. Swanton. London: Phoenix.

The Irish Annals. CODECS: Online Database and e-Resources for Celtic Studies. <http://www.vanhamel.nl/codecs/Category:Irish_annals>.

SECONDARY LITERATURE

Andersen, A., (2010) *Gammel mat og mette*. <http://www.limnoan.no/Vikingmat.pdf>.

Brink, S. (ed.) & Price, N. (ed.) (2008). *The Viking World*. London: Routledge.

Biddle, M., and B. Kjølbye-Biddle (2001). Repton and the 'Great Heathen Army' 873-4, in *Vikings and the Danelaw: Select Papers from the Proceedings of the Thirteenth Viking Congress,* edited by James Graham-Campbell *et al.* Oxford: Oxbow.

Downham, C., (2007). *Viking Kings of Britain and Ireland, The Dynasty of Ívarr to A.D. 1014*. Edinburgh: Dunedin Academic Press.

Forte, A., Oram, R. & Pedersen, F. (2005). *Viking Empires*. Cambridge: Cambridge University Press.

Gardela, L. (2012). What the Vikings did for fun? Sports and pastimes in medieval northern Europe, *World Archaelogy*, 44:2 234–247.

Hem Eriksen, M. (ed.), Pedersen, U. (ed.), Rundberget, B. (ed.), Axelsen, I. (ed.), Lund Berg, H. (ed.) (2015). *Viking Worlds: Things, Spaces and Movement*. Oxford: Oxbow.

Hjardar, K. and Vike, V. (2016) *Vikings at War*. Oxford: Casemate Publishing.

Hjardar, K. (2013) *Vikingenes verden i kart, tekst og bilder*. Oslo: Spartacus.

Hjardar, K. (2001). *Det sakrale kongedømmet i Heimskringla: Om fyrstemakt i vikingtid og middelalder*. Oslo: Illustrert Historie.

Lind, I. (2005). *Norrøn mytologi: Frå A til Å*. Oslo: Samlaget.

Mc Carthy, Daniel P., (2008) *The Irish Annals: their genesis, evolution and history*. Dublin: Four Courts Press.

Steinsland, G. (2005). *Norrøn religion: Myter, riter, samfunn*. Oslo: Pax Forlag.

WEBSITES

Hauge, A., (2002) Arild Hauges runer. Om vikingtid, runer, førkristen tradisjon og folketro i Norden. Danmark, Århus <www.arild-hauge.com>.

INDEX

GLADIATORS

FIGHTING TO THE DEATH IN ANCIENT ROME

M. C. BISHOP

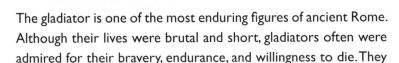

The gladiator is one of the most enduring figures of ancient Rome. Although their lives were brutal and short, gladiators often were admired for their bravery, endurance, and willingness to die. They were the celebrities of their day.

But how did they fight and how did their weapons and techniques develop? Who were they? This book gives an entertaining overview of the history of the gladiator, debunking some myths along the way. We learn about the different forms of combat and the pairings which were designed to carefully balance the strengths and weaknesses of one against the other. This book reveals what we know and how we know it: ancient remains, contemporary sources, graffiti and above all the discovery of gladiator barracks at Pompeii.

M. C. Bishop is a specialist on the Roman army, with many publications to his name including the acclaimed and widely used *Roman Military Equipment* (2006). The founding editor of *Journal of Roman Military Equipment Studies*, he has also led several excavations of Roman sites.

ISBN 9781612005133 • £7.99 • $12.95

GREEK WARRIORS

HOPLITES AND HEROES

CAROLYN WILLEKES

Thermopylae, Marathon: though fought 2,500 years ago in ancient Greece, the names of these battles are more familiar to many than battles fought in the last half-century, but our concept of the men who fought in these battles may be more a product of Hollywood than Greece. Shaped by the landscape in which they fought, the warriors of ancient Greece were mainly heavy infantry. While Bronze Age Greeks fought as individuals, for personal glory, the soldiers of the Classical city states fought as hoplites, armed with long spears and large shields, in an organised formation called the phalanx. This book sketches the change from heroic to hoplite warfare, and discusses the equipment and training of both the citizen soldiers of most Greek cities, and the professional soldiers of Sparta.

Carolyn Willekes is a lecturer based at the University of Calgary. She specializes in Greek history and archaeology, especially the late Classical and Hellenistic periods, with a particular interest in cavalry and horse culture.

ISBN 9781612005157 • £7.99 • $12.95

KNIGHTS

CHIVALRY AND VIOLENCE

JOHN SADLER & ROSIE SERDIVILLE

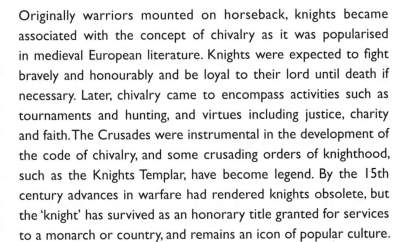

Originally warriors mounted on horseback, knights became associated with the concept of chivalry as it was popularised in medieval European literature. Knights were expected to fight bravely and honourably and be loyal to their lord until death if necessary. Later, chivalry came to encompass activities such as tournaments and hunting, and virtues including justice, charity and faith. The Crusades were instrumental in the development of the code of chivalry, and some crusading orders of knighthood, such as the Knights Templar, have become legend. By the 15th century advances in warfare had rendered knights obsolete, but the 'knight' has survived as an honorary title granted for services to a monarch or country, and remains an icon of popular culture. This short history will cover the rise and decline of the medieval knights, including the extensive training, specific arms and armour, tournaments and the important concept of chivalry.

John Sadler is a military historian living in Northumberland. He is the author of numerous books and also lectures at Newcastle University's Centre for Lifelong Learning. Rosie Serdiville is a social historian and re-enactor with a particular interest in the wider impact of war on civilian populations.

ISBN 9781612005171 • £7.99 • $12.95

FIGHTER ACES

MASTERS OF THE SKIES | JOHN SADLER & ROSIE SERDIVILLE

In 1915 the term 'ace' was coined to denote a pilot adept at downing enemy aircraft, and top aces became household names. This guide offers an accessible history of flying aces, from these first aces in 1915 to the high-powered aerial dogfights of WWII and beyond.

ISBN 9781612004822 • £7.99 • $12.95

TOMMIES

THE BRITISH ARMY IN THE TRENCHES | JOHN SADLER & ROSIE SERDIVILLE

British soldiers have been known as Tommies for centuries, but the name is particularly associated with the British soldier in World War I. This book explores the development of the 'Tommy', presenting the experience of those who lived and died in vast trench systems.

ISBN 9781612004846 • £7.99 • $12.95

SHARPSHOOTERS

MARKSMEN THROUGH THE AGES | GARY YEE

This book looks at marksmen through the ages covering the first serious use of sharpshooters on the battlefield during the Seven Years War, the Napoleonic Wars, the mass-production of high-quality firearms in the mid-19th century, and snipers in World War I.

ISBN 9781612004860 • £7.99 • $12.95

BIG GUNS

ARTILLERY ON THE BATTLEFIELD | ANGUS KONSTAM

Big Guns covers use of artillery over the centuries including the cannons initially developed to tackle fortifications, the development of lighter, more manoeuvrable field artillery that would come to change the outcome of battles, and its central role in modern warfare.

ISBN 9781612004884 • £7.99 • $12.95

TANKS

A CENTURY OF TANK WARFARE | OSCAR E. GILBERT & ROMAIN CANSIERE

From the slow and clumsy Mark IV, through the terrifying Tiger and nimble Sherman Firefly to the Challenger 2, this book covers the development of tanks, and how they have been used in warfare through the two world wars and beyond.

ISBN 9781612004907 • £7.99 • $12.95